DR. LONNIE E. RILEY

THE
EXTRAORDINARY
POWER OF

1%

40 Motivational Studies

That Can Change Your Life

1% At A Time.

Cover Design: Kimberly T. Riley

Published in 2012 by
Freedom Place Publishing
2607 Yaupon Drive #2
Myrtle Beach, SC 29577
www.thefreedomcenteronline.org

All Scripture references are taken from The Message, *(MSG)*
Copyright © 1993, 1994, 1995, 1996, 2000, 2001, 2002
by Eugene H. Peterson

Library of Congress Control Number: 2012952758

Printed in the United States of America

CONTENTS

<u>Dedication</u>

I dedicate this book to my loving mother,

Ann Wiggins.

She is the one Godly, consistent person in my life over these 50+ years. She has always been there for me, even when I messed up royally.

She has challenged and motivated me to incrementally change into the man I am today.

Thank you for what you have taught me, Mom.

I Love You

Foreword

As time moves on, it seems as if the world is moving at a much faster pace. The dozens of various technologies that we surround our lives with are constantly pushing us in a multitude of directions. Then of course there are the countless activities that we fill our lives with, so that, perhaps, we can gain a sense of accomplishment. However, it is important, at various stages in life, to step aside from the hustle and bustle of the world, and see what we have actually accomplished, and to hone in on what our lives have been focused on.

As believers in Christ, our primary focus should of course be on building our relationship with Him. We as Christians are not meant to say a humble prayer of repentance and acceptance, then abandon the very One who saved us. Rather, we are meant to pursue a deep and purposeful relationship with our Savior, our Creator.

How then can we build this relationship with all of the activities of life pulling us in every direction? Well, the first step is to devote a period of time, no matter how small at first, and in that time seek out to build that important relationship with Christ. To be truly successful in this life, a believer must live with Christ as their central focus. Just as a marital relationship requires constant work and devotion, so does our relationship with Christ. Sometimes however, just as in other aspects in life, we need a guide, a helping hand, in order to build and hone such a relationship.

This is the exact purpose of this devotional. Through the various weeks involved, you will gain very important perspectives on your relationship with Christ. You will see who you are to Him, what He has planned and purposed for you, and how you are to share that life and love with others. While this devotional will not suffice to stabilize your relationship with Christ forever, it will undoubtedly assist in building a solid foundation.

The thought provoking questions on each day force you to truly think about the various aspects of your relationship with Christ, and the split morning/night sessions allow Christ to be central on your heart and mind throughout the day. I truly hope that you are able to use this book for all it is worth. If you are honest, and seek after Christ with a pure heart during this devotional, I believe He will come to you, and your relationship with Him will begin to blossom.

When you are finished with the book, do not just push it to the back of your library and confine it to solitude and abandonment. Rather, set it aside for a half a year, then come back to it, and see how your relationship with Christ, and others, has grown and matured. Then go through it again. Use it constantly as a guide in building a truly lasting relationship with Christ. In the course of this book, I pray that you grow deeper in love with Christ, and live your life with Him as your true focus.

-- Jason M. Riley, MA

Preface

The mind is a powerful thing. We become what we focus our mind upon. That being said, it only makes sense to purposely set our mind on good, positive and holy things. The world in which we live thrives on the negative. One only has to watch the news to realize that. Our jobs are often negative in that we hear little praise but reprimands are quick and hurtful. Some churches even build their message on the negative things in the Bible. Yet I believe God wants His children to be people of faith, hope and love. I have written this to help turn you into that type of person. Positive. Hopeful. Loving. Faithful.

Most of us want to change our lives for the better. We really desire to be all that God has intended for us. We know what type of person we should be, but the task seems insurmountable. After serving in differing ministry positions over 30 years, I have seen the need first hand. People need encouragement! If you have been following Jesus Christ for long, most of the truths in this book will not be new to you. I don't think that we lack the knowledge; we have lacked the formula for putting the knowledge into action.

When that formula is available, we need encouragement in the daily grind of implementing it. That is what I wish to do for you! I pray that each day during these 40 studies you will be challenged and encouraged. You will become the optimistic, powerful, confident, expectant person you know God intended for you to be.

It only takes small changes to reap large results. If you are married, you know this truth I'm speaking about. You made one, simple decision and it has changed the rest of your life. All decisions, plans, possibilities and problems have been affected by this one decision. So it is with your decision to become a disciple of Jesus Christ. This impacted your future both on earth and for eternity. This truth is the basis for these studies. One truth that is accepted, internalized and practice can change your life.

Consider this. If you're going somewhere and you're off course by just one degree, after one foot, you'll miss your target by 0.2 inches. Trivial, right? But what about as you get farther out?

- After 100 yards, you'll be off by 5.2 feet. Not huge, but noticeable.
- After a mile, you'll be off by 92.2 feet. One degree is starting to make a difference.
- After traveling from San Francisco to L.A., you'll be off by 6 miles.
- If you were trying to get from San Francisco to Washington, D.C., you'd end up on the other side of Baltimore, 42.6 miles away.
- Traveling around the globe from Washington, DC, you'd miss by 435 miles and end up in Boston.
- In a rocket going to the moon, you'd be 4,169 miles off (nearly twice the diameter of the moon).
- Going to the sun, you'd miss by over 1.6 million miles (nearly twice the diameter of the sun).
- Traveling to the nearest star, you'd be off course by over 441 billion miles (120 times the distance from the earth to Pluto, or 4,745 times the distance from Earth to the sun).

Over time, a mere one percent change in course makes a huge difference! The longer you stay with a small change you it is no longer insignificant or inconsequential.

Think of it this way, at 211 degrees, water is hot. Yet one degree hotter at 212 degrees, it boils. See the difference?

This book does not promise to create a new person out of you by the end of 40 days. It does promise to help you make some important small course directions that can ultimately impact your life. Just a one percent change can alter your destiny and create a totally new goal for your final destination. I pray that this will be the case for you as you push through these studies.

By working each day through the topic and really trying to put it into practice, you will experience the impact it can have on your life. The subject which really touches you, that "Aha" moment, is an area where you can begin developing and begin the 1% change in that portion of your life.

A work like this doesn't come about easily. I am indebted to many as it has taken time and effort to compile these thoughts. Here are those to whom I feel I need to express my gratitude.

God is my number one fan, and I thank Him so much for helping me through this project. He is my Source and I rely solely on Him. He has helped me change in these areas and placed the desire within me to share these concepts with you.

My wonderful wife, Kim, is a constant and faithful encouragement to me. She always sees the positive in me and my abilities. She has been my editor, proof reader, and designer. Nothing I do would be near this quality without her involvement.

Thanks to my oldest son, Jason. An up and coming scholar in his own right as he prepares to begin his studies for a PhD took the time to read through my rough drafts, editing, proofing and offering suggestions on layout and presentation along the way. His willingness to write the foreword gives me great joy.

I am so grateful to the congregation I serve, The Freedom Center Church, for all that they do for me. They are a wonderful group of positive influential people with dynamic faith in Christ Jesus. The contents of this book are a result of a series of messages received by them in an effort to activate their walk with God in a positive, life-changing way. I love all of you.

Last, but definitely not least, I thank you, the reader. I appreciate the fact that you bought this book. More importantly, I thank you for making the investment in yourself. I am pleased that you have decided to embark on this journey with me. I celebrate the person I believe God wants you to become. I truly hope (confident expectation) that you experience the change God desires for you.

Prayer: *Heavenly Father, I want to ask You for Your guidance and power as this reader begins this book. I pray for Your Holy Spirit to quicken what is appropriate for them in their own personal life. Transform them into the positive and powerful person of faith that You have intended for them to be. Lead them as they understand Your eternal purpose for their life. And then, may they become a catalyst for change in those over whom they have influence. I leave all this at Your feet and trust You with the results. AMEN*

How To Use This Book

The format for each of the 40 days is the same. Begin each day by stopping and asking God to speak to you during this time. Let the positive statement for the day sink into your mind. Read the morning Scripture that is provided and consider how you can make it applicable.

Next read the short lesson. Following the lesson you will find a section called "Prayer Starter." This is just a short prayer I have included to help your process of focusing on this topic during your prayers. Use it as a starter, NOT your entire prayer time. Listen for God's voice in your mind and respond like any other conversation you might have.

Then the Positive Statement for the Day is what you will take with you and focus on thinking about and saying it all day long. Some of the statements speak of what you will do that day. Look for every opportunity to accomplish the task and watch as it begins to transform you.

At the end of the day, there is a "check-up" on your experience using the statement for the day for review and a final prayer starter. Review how God has used this statement throughout your day to begin to alter your life. Answer the few questions and then use the final "Prayer Starter" as a launching pad for a time of intimate conversation with your Heavenly Father at the end of your day.

Suggested uses for
THE EXTRAORDINARY POWER OF 1%

✓ **Personal Study:** This is perfect for daily reading and encouragement as you develop spiritually in your personal life. Working through the book will challenge you to make incremental changes in your life and keep you focused on becoming the godly person you really desire to be.

✓ **Group Study:** How awesome it is when like-minded believers share a journey together. Your group, men's or women's ministry, small group meetings or even mid-week bible studies can use this book as a catalyst to move the entire group toward positive change and maturity. Great testimonies will follow and real life change will happen in an accountable and methodical fashion.

✓ **Youth Format:** Use this book as a way of producing authentic Christian community within your youth group. Follow it week by week over 40 weeks. It will keep your group focused and generate real enthusiasm for how God can develop them into strong and genuine Disciples of Christ. They will be excited as they experience and observe both their own personal change, and the change that happens in their friends. Contagious change that will lift the entire moral of the group.

Blessings on you as you begin this incredible, life-changing journey.

Section 1

MOTIVATED
To Change

Day One

Morning

Positive Statement for the Day:

I Will Make One Small Change Toward Godliness

2 Peter 1:5-9

"So don't lose a minute in building on what you've been given, complementing your basic faith with good character, spiritual understanding, alert discipline, passionate patience, reverent wonder, warm friendliness, and generous love, each dimension fitting into and developing the others. With these qualities active and growing in your lives, no grass will grow under your feet, no day will pass without its reward as you mature in your experience of our Master Jesus. Without these qualities you can't see what's right before you, oblivious that your old sinful life has been wiped off the books."

Change is never easy in our life, unless the pain of change is less than the pain of staying the way we are. We are creatures of habit. We have formed these habits over the years, and after that they begin to form us. That's a hard truth, but once understood can help us understand ourselves.

One small change in any area of our life, business, or family can make a lasting impact. Even if you just change one habit, it can potentially transform your life. Change is that potent. It is so powerful that it can totally alter the direction of your life.

If you will change, even one small thing in your life, you will begin to see a ripple effect that will eventually change you. Just one new habit will affect you, not only now, but also for years to come.

If you will make a small, incremental change in your attitude toward growing in your Christian walk each week, by the end of a year you will have experienced huge growth. The reason it is so powerful is that it compounds over time and creates a new paradigm in that area of your life.

Did you know that if you were to fly a plane but were off course by just 1 degree, that for every mile you travel that way you get 92 feet further away from your destination. If you started at the equator and wanted to fly around the world, but you were 1 degree off, you would land 500 miles off target. Now you can visualize the extraordinary power of changing just 1%.

So, how do you start this journey toward change? Do a self-evaluation. Ask God's Spirit to guide you. Find a degree of change that you can make. Perhaps it will be one of the positive statements for the day you will be using in this book. Then commit to making that one degree of change in your life with God's help. Then again, you may already know areas that are screaming for change in your life

Like I have said before, "Change one habit and change your life."

Prayer Starter

God, show me where I can make real change in my life so that I may be more like Jesus. Point out the areas in my actions and attitudes where I can incrementally adjust my heading so that I become a better witness for You. AMEN

"Check Up"

1. How have you experience the power of positive change in your life in the past?

    _____

    _____

2. Where in your daily living can you make one degree of positive change?

    _____

    _____

3. When will you make the commitment to begin the process of changing that one area?

    _____

    _____

4. What observations did you make today while focusing on today's statement: I will make one small change toward Godliness?

    _____

    _____

    _____

    _____

    _____

    _____

Prayer Starter

Thank You, Father, for a day of revelation. You revealed areas in my life that I can change with Your help. Give me strength and determination to make at least one small change in those areas. Create a desire to see how You will work that transformation for my good. AMEN

Day Two

Morning

Positive Statement for the Day:

I Will Make Time
To Spend With God

Psalm 1:2
Instead you thrill to GOD's Word,
you chew on Scripture day and night.

Psalm 5:1-3
Listen, GOD! Please, pay attention!
Can you make sense of these ramblings,
my groans and cries?
King-God, I need your help.
Every morning you'll hear me at it again.
Every morning I lay out the pieces of my life
on your altar and watch for fire to descend.

Psalm 55:16-17
I call to God;
GOD will help me.
At dusk, dawn, and noon I sigh
deep sighs—he hears, he rescues.

Psalm 88:13
I'm standing my ground, GOD,
shouting for help,
at my prayers every morning,
on my knees each daybreak.

If you really want to take this Christian life seriously, if you are truly thankful for the salvation God has provided for you and if you honestly desire to advance the Kingdom of God, then you need to spend time with Him.

Jesus wants to do more than save you. He desires to teach you, heal you, deliver you, encourage you, lift you up, and just love on you. His longing is to spend quality, intimate, soul searching time with you.

Listen carefully to me now, this is important. For the devoted child of God, nothing (not – a - thing) is more important in your life than your time alone with God. No possession is as essential. No job is as vital. No person or relationship is more critical.

You have to make it a priority, a planned daily appointment. It should take precedence over everything else in your schedule. If you are too busy to spend time with Jesus, adjust your priorities. If you are too tired to get alone with God, then get some rest. And if you are just too lazy to spend time with your Savior, get some accountability. It is that important.

It is so essential, that you will face temptation to keep from being constant and consistent. It takes a deep desire and a total commitment in order to make it a real priority. Commit yourself to a daily time alone with God.

Prayer Starter
Father, I know that I need to make it a priority to meet with You every day. I confess that I have not always been faithful to our time together. Forgive me, Lord, and always remind me that You want to spend time with me also. AMEN

"Check Up"

1. What has kept you from having a daily time alone with God?

   _____

   _____

2. Since you realize the importance of your time with God, when will your daily appointment be?

   _____

   _____

3. Knowing this appointment is about building a relationship with God, how will you spend this time?

   _____

   _____

4. What observations did you make today while focusing on today's statement: I will make time to spend with God ?

   _____

   _____

   _____

   _____

   _____

   _____

Prayer Starter

Lord, I am so excited about spending time with You each and every day. I know that our relationship is going to flourish. We are going to be closer than we've ever been. I am going to see You work in my life like never before. Thank You for revealing this to me. AMEN

Day Three

Morning

Positive Statement for the Day:

I Will Be Aware Of God's Voice

1 Kings 19:11-13

Then he was told, "Go, stand on the mountain at attention before GOD. GOD will pass by."

A hurricane wind ripped through the mountains and shattered the rocks before GOD, but GOD wasn't to be found in the wind; after the wind an earthquake, but GOD wasn't in the earthquake; and after the earthquake fire, but GOD wasn't in the fire; and after the fire a gentle and quiet whisper.

When Elijah heard the quiet voice, he muffled his face with his great cloak, went to the mouth of the cave, and stood there. A quiet voice asked, "So Elijah, now tell me, what are you doing here?"

Sometimes we may actually hear something without really listening. I remember, especially as a teenager, that I did that often, both at home and also at school. I can remember my mother telling me things, but I was not really listening to the details. I guess that's one of the reasons I found myself in trouble.

Hearing is not the same as listening. To listen requires concentration and attention to detail. It necessitates that we be engaged in the conversation. It involves absorbing not only the words, but also their intent and their context.

God desires to speak with you today. Yes, He is concerned with your requests, but He wants to do more than listen to the recitation of your list to Him. He wants to communicate with you. Will you listen?

Does He speak audibly? I would have to say yes, though I have never heard Him myself. Most often I think you will be able to recognize His voice through the Bible, through others, through your circumstances, and especially through the Holy Spirit as the *inner voice* that will lead you.

Just like you can recognize your closest family and friend's voice on the telephone, you can learn to recognize the voice of God in your life. He wants that type of relationship with you.

He wants you to hear Him. The God of the universe has something to say to you. Your Creator desires an intimate connection where both of you recognize each other's voice. Where you build a bond, a link, or a rapport that is supernatural.

Prayer Starter

Lord Jesus, I desperately desire to have the type of relationship with You where I recognize Your voice. Teach me how to hear Your words. Show me how to tune out the other voices of the world so I can focus on Yours. I know I can do this with Your help. AMEN

"Check Up"

1. What other "voices" in your life do you allow to drown out the voice of God?

_____

_____

2. In reflecting over your walk with God, how has He most effectively spoken to you?

_____

_____

3. How will you make time in your schedule to actually listen for the voice of God?

_____

_____

4. What observations did you make today while focusing on today's statement: I will be aware of God's voice?

_____

_____

_____

_____

_____

_____

Prayer Starter

Thank You, Lord, for speaking to me throughout this day. I can see now how this is supposed to work. You want to communicate with me all day, not just when I stop and read the Bible. It may take me some time to develop, but help me learn how to distinguish Your voice from all the noise of the world. AMEN

Day Four

Morning

Positive Statement for the Day:

I Will Internalize God's Word

Psalm 119:11
*I've banked your promises in the vault of my heart
so I won't sin myself bankrupt.*

Psalm 119:105
*By your words I can see where I'm going;
they throw a beam of light on my dark path.*

Hebrews 4:12-13
*God means what he says. What he says goes.
His powerful Word is sharp as a surgeon's scalpel,
cutting through everything, whether doubt or defense, laying
us open to listen and obey.
Nothing and no one is impervious to God's Word.
We can't get away from it—no matter what.*

The word of God is powerful. He created all things by the Word of His mouth. The written word is a revelation of God and His purposes over all time. Our first scripture focuses on the power of internalizing the word of God as a deterrent from sin. We have an example in Jesus.

When Jesus was tempted, His response to all three temptations was, "It is written." He didn't use His power as the 2nd person of the Trinity. He didn't create a miracle or a smoke screen. He quoted the Word of God that He had internalized.

OK, that sounds good, doesn't it? You need to do that, don't you? So, how do you internalize His word? It sounds good, but how do you do it?

You begin by actually reading the Bible. I know that at times that can seem like a chore. Find a version of the Bible that you more easily understand. Maybe even a paraphrase would help you understand what you are reading. Now, begin studying it. The Bible calls this meditating on what you have learned. See how what you have read fits into the whole scheme of Scripture. Memorize small sections or verses.

Next, you start to use it in your daily life. Be obedient to what the word says. Put your faith into practice by making that word part of you. Begin sharing how it has made a difference in your walk with God.

Then, the next step is to teach what you have learned so that others can be blessed by what you have learned. When you prepare to teach something, you really begin to learn even more.

If you do these things, you will develop a strong desire to know more and to apply it to your daily living.

Prayer Starter
Heavenly Father, give me a desire and a love for Your word. Help me to hide Your word in my heart, that I might not sin against You. AMEN

"Check Up"

1. What part of the Bible will you begin to read and study?

_____

_____

2. What verses or sections of the Bible do you intend to commit to memory?

_____

_____

3. When will you step up and volunteer to teach a section or topic from the Bible?

_____

_____

4. What observations did you make today while focusing on today's statement: I will internalize God's word?

_____

_____

_____

_____

_____

_____

Prayer Starter

Your word, oh Lord, is indeed a lamp to my feet And a light to my path. I can see the importance of internalizing Your word. Thank You for creating in me a yearning to learn more of Your truth. Make me into a walking, talking student of Your precious promises. AMEN

Day Five

Morning

Positive Statement for the Day:

I Will Be Quick To Obey God's Promptings

John 14:23-24
"Because a loveless world," said Jesus,
"is a sightless world. If anyone loves me, he will carefully keep
my word and my Father will love him—we'll move right into
the neighborhood!
Not loving me means not keeping my words.
The message you are hearing isn't mine.
It's the message of the Father who sent me.

1 Peter 1:22-23
Now that you've cleaned up your lives by following the truth,
love one another as if your lives depended on it.
Your new life is not like your old life.
Your old birth came from mortal sperm;
your new birth comes from God's living Word

Jesus made it very clear that if we are His disciples, we will obey His commands. Not out of fear of hell or punishment, but out of love. Every act of obedience builds a tender heart toward God. Likewise, every act of disobedience builds a hard heart.

The first miracle performed by Jesus was turning the water into wine at a wedding in Cana of Galilee (John 2:1-11).

His mother, Mary, told the servants to do whatever Jesus told them to do (obedience). They obeyed and Jesus was able to perform the miracle.

I've often wondered if they didn't obey, if there would have been a miracle at all. They held the key, through their obedience, to the great miracle. And the miracle wasn't even for them; it was for the couple being married.

Do you realize that you could be holding the key to a miracle in either your life or someone else's life by your obedience? Jesus may just be waiting on you to step up and obey His word so that He can show God's glory in some situation around you.

In the armed forces of America, boot camp is time of intense preparation. Part of the process is designed to break the individual of questioning or disobeying an order. Service men and women are trained to obey each and every order without question.

You need to be trained with that obedient focus toward God and His word. You must cultivate a mental attitude of quick and prompt obedience to God.

Prayer Starter

Dear Jesus, I want to be quick to obey Your promptings in my life. I want to always keep the flow of divine power at work in my life. I desire to give You every opportunity to show Yourself strong in the world through my prompt obedience to You. AMEN

"Check Up"

1. What areas of truth from God's word have you NOT been quick to obey?

_____

_____

2. What rationalizations have you used to justify your disobedience?

_____

_____

3. How will you turn (repent) from your disobedience and begin to follow the word?

_____

_____

4. What observations did you make today while focusing on today's statement: I will be quick to obey God's promptings?

_____

_____

_____

_____

_____

_____

Prayer Starter

Lord, it feels good to be obedient to Your word. I regret that I haven't been quicker at responding to the truths You have shown me in the past. I am committing myself to You in a fresh way from this point forward. I will obey, regardless of my feelings or excuses. AMEN

Section 2

MOTIVATED
By The Power Of The Spirit

Day Six

Morning

Positive Statement for the Day:

God Wants To Immerse Me With His Holy Spirit

Acts 1:4-8
As they met and ate meals together,
he told them that they were on no account to leave Jerusalem
but "must wait for what the Father promised: the promise you
heard from me.
John baptized in water;
you will be baptized in the Holy Spirit. And soon."

When they were together for the last time they asked, "Master,
are you going to restore the kingdom to Israel now? Is this the
time?"

He told them, "You don't get to know the time. Timing is the
Father's business. What you'll get is the Holy Spirit.

And when the Holy Spirit comes on you, you will be able to be
my witnesses in Jerusalem, all over Judea and Samaria, even
to the ends of the world."

Jesus told His disciples that it was to their advantage that He leave and re-join the Father in heaven. It was hard for them to understand.

They sacrificed their lives to follow Him, and they thought He would set up His kingdom on earth. Now He is saying that He is leaving and that it would profit them more if He did. Why? Jesus knew that, as one Man, He could only influence and guide a select few; but by sending the Holy Spirit, He could live within and help all believers.

In the Old Testament only a select few were given the Holy Spirit to help them with their ministry. But the prophet Joel spoke of a time when God would pour His Spirit on all flesh; when sons and daughters would prophecy. When young men would see visions and old men would dream dreams. Even the servants would receive this outpouring and also prophecy.

In Acts 1, Jesus tells the disciples He is going to baptize them with the Holy Spirit. He planned to immerse them in the power and presence of God through His Spirit.

You can also have this type of experience. God wants to immerse (baptize) you in this glorious encounter with the Holy Spirit so that you are equipped from within to live the Christian life.

He is waiting to do this for you, if you will ask.

Prayer Starter
Lord, I realize that You are wanting to baptize me with Your Holy Spirit. I submit myself to You. Your will. Your divine purpose. I need this power and presence in my life. I expect to receive it in Jesus name. AMEN

"Check Up"

1. How can you see the baptism of the Holy Spirit changing your life?

_____

_____

2. If you have not received this baptism separate from salvation, why haven't you?

_____

_____

3. God promises this baptism with the Holy Spirit, so what is stopping you from receiving it now, today?

_____

_____

4. What observations did you make today while focusing on today's statement: God wants to immerse me with His Holy Spirit?

_____

_____

_____

_____

_____

Prayer Starter

Thank You, Lord, for the promise of sending Your Holy Spirit. I know I need this. I must have it. I can't continue in my walk with Christ without it. I will not rest until I have the assurance of being baptized with Your Holy Spirit. Cleanse my thought and actions. I will continually seek and ask until I receive. AMEN

Day Seven

Morning

Positive Statement for the Day:

I Run To Jesus To Receive The Holy Spirit

John 16:4-15

I didn't tell you this earlier because I was with you every day. But now I am on my way to the One who sent me. Not one of you has asked, 'Where are you going?' Instead, the longer I've talked, the sadder you've become. So let me say it again, this truth: It's better for you that I leave. If I don't leave, the Friend won't come. But if I go, I'll send him to you.

"When he comes, he'll expose the error of the godless world's view of sin, righteousness, and judgment: He'll show them that their refusal to believe in me is their basic sin; that righteousness comes from above, where I am with the Father, out of their sight and control; that judgment takes place as the ruler of this godless world is brought to trial and convicted.

"I still have many things to tell you, but you can't handle them now. But when the Friend comes, the Spirit of the Truth, he will take you by the hand and guide you into all the truth there is. He won't draw attention to himself, but will make sense out of what is about to happen and, indeed, out of all that I have done and said. He will honor me; he will take from me and deliver it to you. Everything the Father has is also mine. That is why I've said, 'He takes from me and delivers to you.'

Jesus is the Giver of the Holy Spirit. He is the Baptizer. He is the Officiate. To receive the Holy Spirit you have to receive from Jesus.

This is of vital importance to your successful Christian life. It is something you need AFTER you have become a Christian. It brings about an empowerment that helps you be His witness and to live a holy and pure life.

Run to Jesus. Don't wait any longer. Run. Make this a priority in your life. Surrender everything fresh and new to God and open your spirit for a full immersion of His Spirit.

You can live a life of holiness before God, but not in your own strength. You need the power of His Spirit to sanctify you (set you apart as His vessel). The powerful, cleansing work that God intends for you to experience is waiting for you. He wants you to have it. He designed that you be able to receive it.

Don't wait any longer. Stop living a defeated Christian life by trying to do it in your own strength. Run to Jesus now! Let Him give you the awesome gift of the Holy Spirit. Surrender yourself to His Lordship.

Prayer Starter
Jesus, I run to You now. I surrender all that I am, all that I have and all of my future to You. Pour out Your Holy Spirit on me even now. Cleanse me from my ungodly carnality and fill me with Your perfect love. AMEN

"Check Up"

1. Why do you think the gift of the Holy Spirit is so vitally important?

_____

_____

2. How can you see your spiritual life changing if you receive this gift from Jesus?

_____

_____

3. Why did Jesus say it was so important that we receive the gift of the Holy Spirit?

_____

_____

4. What observations did you make today while focusing on today's statement: I run to Jesus to receive the Holy Spirit?

_____

_____

_____

_____

_____

Prayer Starter

Thank You, Lord Jesus, for pouring Your Holy Spirit on me. I have needed this in my life. I know that I am becoming the child of God You intended for me to be through this fresh anointing. The Holy Spirit is now directing, guiding, and controlling my life. I will never be the same. AMEN

Day Eight

Morning

Positive Statement for the Day:

Today, I Will Drink Of The Holy Spirit

John 7:37-39
*On the final and climactic day of the Feast,
Jesus took his stand.
He cried out, "If anyone thirsts, let him come to me and drink.
Rivers of living water will brim and spill out of the depths of
anyone who believes in me this way, just as the Scripture
says."
(He said this in regard to the Spirit, whom those who believed
in him were about to receive. The Spirit had not yet been given
because Jesus had not yet been glorified.)*

Have you ever been really thirsty? Maybe you have
worked out in the hot, blazing sun and after a few hours your
body has used up its available liquids and you just HAVE to
get something to drink. Your body is dehydrated and you
drink and drink in order to replenish it.

Imagine someone lost in the desert. No water in site;
nothing but endless sand and scorching heat. The temperature
rises quickly. You have to get out of there or die. You are
pushing yourself toward civilization. The harder you work at
it, the more energy you use. Your body is perspiring in order
to cool off, so your fluids are diminishing. You are becoming
dehydrated. You've got to find some type of water, even if

it's from the root of a plant. You have to get something to drink.

In your spiritual walk, there may be times of dryness. Times when you are pushing forward by faith, but the world and its pressures are leaving you parched, spiritually dehydrated.

You must purposefully take time to drink of the Holy Spirit fresh and new so that you can continue. Only the refreshing, revitalizing flow of the living water of the Spirit will restore you and invigorate your spirit.

Are you dry today?

Are you running on empty?

Are you pushing through in your own strength?

Are you at the point of spiritual dehydration?

Run to Jesus for the living water He promised to those who believe in Him. Run today. Run now! Open the dry cistern of your heart and drink in of the Holy Spirit. Be refreshed. Be renewed. Be restored. Be empowered. Do it now!

Prayer Starter
God, my Father, I need a fresh drink of Your Holy Spirit today. I make the decision to open up and allow You to pour in me a refreshing, rejuvenating, restoring drink of Your Holy Spirit. AMEN

"Check Up"

1. What things have happened that caused you to spiritually dry up?

   _____

   _____

2. How has the dryness of your soul affected your service for God?

   _____

   _____

3. Now is your time for refreshing. What will you do to have the living water of the Spirit fill your spirit?

   _____

   _____

4. What observations did you make today while focusing on today's statement: Today, I will drink of the Holy Spirit ?

   _____

   _____

   _____

   _____

   _____

Prayer Starter

Wow, Lord. I never realize how parched and dry my soul was. I needed this fresh drink of the living water of Your Spirit. Thank You, Jesus. Please keep me under the flow. I don't ever want to be that dry again. I want to live each day filled to overflowing. AMEN

Day Nine

Morning

Positive Statement for the Day:

I Expect To Be Led By The Holy Spirit

Romans 8:12-17

So don't you see that we don't owe this old do-it-yourself life one red cent. There's nothing in it for us, nothing at all. The best thing to do is give it a decent burial and get on with your new life. God's Spirit beckons. There are things to do and places to go!

This resurrection life you received from God is not a timid, grave-tending life. It's adventurously expectant, greeting God with a childlike "What's next, Papa?" God's Spirit touches our spirits and confirms who we really are. We know who he is, and we know who we are: Father and children. And we know we are going to get what's coming to us—an unbelievable inheritance! We go through exactly what Christ goes through. If we go through the hard times with him, then we're certainly going to go through the good times with him!

There is an old saying, "You can lead a horse to water, but you can't make him drink." We've talked about drinking of the Holy Spirit in our lives so that we are refreshed and revitalized to live a pure and holy life before God, as well as empowered for His service. Yet sometimes, there are things that will stop the flow of this living water from working in us.

One of the ways we can dam up that flow of the Spirit is to be disobedient to His leadings. He wants to guide you through each day. He is our Comforter, our Teacher, our Counselor, and our Guide.

Expect that He will motivate you to holiness. Anticipate that He will lead you toward a productive life. He will gently guide you in the ways of godliness and purity. He will open doors of effective service for you. You don't have to "make" things happen; you just need to be obedient to what the Holy Spirit and God's word says to you.

His inner voice will act not only as a conscience, but also as a tender prompting to lead you in a sanctified, set-apart, and holy life. Living by faith is a life of anticipation and excitement as you learn to lean upon God, obey His commands, and watch Him develop you into the person He as designed for you to be.

You should expect to hear His voice. You should expect for His powerful hand to move things in your favor and to bless you. He is there for you. His plans and thoughts for you are good at all times. He was given to the church (you) for this distinct purpose.

Prayer Starter

I thank You, dear Lord, for the leading of Your Spirit today. I do not assume to have it all together or that I know what I should do today. I will expect the Holy Spirit to inspire me through His gentle leadings today. AMEN

"Check Up"

1. What areas of disobedience have dammed the flow of the Spirit in your life?

    _____

    _____

2. When will you confess the above areas of disobedience to God and open yourself for His guidance?

    _____

    _____

3. How has the Holy Spirit directed your steps in the past?

    _____

    _____

4. What observations did you make today while focusing on today's statement: I expect to be led by the Holy Spirit?

    _____

    _____

    _____

    _____

    _____

Prayer Starter

I have learned today that if I will expect Your leading, You are faithful to do so. Thank You for guiding me all day today. I realize that I can have this type of help and direction every day. I don't have to wing it alone. You are my Helper and my Guide. AMEN

Day Ten

Morning

Positive Statement for the Day:

I Yield My Life To The Holy Spirit

Acts 8:26-28

Later God's angel spoke to Philip: "At noon today I want you to walk over to that desolate road that goes from Jerusalem down to Gaza." He got up and went. He met an Ethiopian eunuch coming down the road. The eunuch had been on a pilgrimage to Jerusalem and was returning to Ethiopia, where he was minister in charge of all the finances of Candace, queen of the Ethiopians. He was riding in a chariot and reading the prophet Isaiah.

Acts 8:38-40

As they continued down the road, they came to a stream of water. The eunuch said, "Here's water. Why can't I be baptized?" He ordered the chariot to stop. They both went down to the water, and Philip baptized him on the spot. When they came up out of the water, the Spirit of God suddenly took Philip off, and that was the last the eunuch saw of him. But he didn't mind. He had what he'd come for and went on down the road as happy as he could be.

Philip showed up in Azotus and continued north, preaching the Message in all the villages along that route until he arrived at Caesarea.

I live right off of the outer loop (bypass) around Charlotte, NC. It is a very busy road nearly all the time. There are some times when the traffic comes to a slow crawl. Specifically, coming off of the interstate during the evening around 5:00 to 7:00 it almost totally stops.

I used to think the problem was careless drivers running into each other. Yet, each time I sat through this traffic, there was no wreck to be found. I then realized it was because of poor planning. The road changes from an eight lane to a four lane at a place where some of the busiest exits pour into the road. In short, it's almost always merging traffic. It slows down because others have to yield the right of way.

From this real life object lesson, I have learned that we also must yield the right of way to the Holy Spirit of God.

You should slow down and defer to His movement in your life. His will and His plan should always cause you to surrender or give way to Him. He sees the big picture. He knows of the incidents ahead. He will guide you on the "alternate route" you must take to avoid an accident.

"I surrender all, to You my Lord and King,
Everything I am and all I'll ever be.
I surrender all my silent hopes and dreams.
I surrender all, I surrender all"

Prayer Starter
I yield my life today to Your Spirit, Father. I submit my plans and will rearrange my life to follow Him. I want to be led through the congestion of my life. I want to avoid the possible accidents ahead of me. I totally submit to Your yield signs. AMEN

"Check Up"

1. What areas of your life have remained un-yielded to the Holy Spirit's control?

_____

_____

2. Why have you resisted God's call to surrender those areas of your life to Him?

_____

_____

3. What specific area in your life did you surrender today?

_____

_____

4. What observations did you make today while focusing on today's statement: I yield my life to the Holy Spirit?

_____

_____

_____

_____

_____

Prayer Starter

Lord, as I have submitted my own plans today and yielded my life fresh to You, I have understood the power of surrender. You are the strength of my life and I thank You for revealing that truth to me in such tangible ways today. AMEN

Section 3

MOTIVATED
By Who I Am In Christ

Day Eleven

Morning

Positive Statement for the Day:

God Accepts And Approves Of Me

Ephesians 1:3-6

How blessed is God!
And what a blessing he is!
He's the Father of our Master, Jesus Christ,
and takes us to the high places of blessing in him.
Long before he laid down earth's foundations,
he had us in mind, had settled on us as the focus of his love, to
be made whole and holy by his love.
Long, long ago he decided to adopt us into his family through
Jesus Christ.
(What pleasure he took in planning this!)
He wanted us to enter into the celebration of his lavish
gift-giving by the hand of his beloved Son.

Everyone wants to be accepted by others. We all desire approval. We start our lives as little children wanting approval and acceptance from our family. School somehow seems to fertilize that desire and as we progress into middle school and on to high school we crave it even more.

Usually that acceptance and approval is tied to what we do. Sometimes by what we don't or won't do.

We develop a performance mind-set in order to win that recognition from those we care about.

Our job performance or status in life is often directly related to our feelings of acceptance and approval. If we perform well, do our jobs right, go the extra mile, and put in the extra hours, perhaps we will be recognized or even promoted.

God is different. You cannot win His approval. You cannot earn His acceptance. He knows you. He understands you better than anyone on this earth. He knows your deepest secrets and darkest thoughts. The Scripture reminds us that man looks on the outward appearance and performance, but God looks at our heart.

Let me remind you today, that in spite of your flaws, mistakes and sins, He loves you. He accepts you, just as you are. God approves of you, without your having to earn it. He loves you perfectly. You cannot earn acceptance into heaven based on your works or your perceived worth. Salvation is through faith alone. Faith in what Christ Jesus did for you.

He is Your heavenly Father. He is the perfect example of what a Father should be. He is not judging you. The time for that will come, but not now. He loves you unconditionally and is totally on your side. There is nothing you can do to make Him love you more, and nothing you can do to make Him love you less.

Prayer Starter

Father, thank You for accepting me as I am. Your approval means more to me than any person on this earth. I know You love me, and that You love me enough to help me change where I can to become more like You. Amen

"Check Up"

1. In what ways have you realized you were trying to earn God's approval or acceptance?

_____

_____

2. Have you been overly concerned with earning the approval or acceptance of others? If so name them.

_____

_____

3. What can you do to minimize the problem of seeking acceptance and approval from man?

_____

_____

4. What observations did you make today while focusing on today's statement: God accepts and approves of me?

_____

_____

_____

_____

_____

_____

_____

Prayer Starter

I praise You, O God, for the realization that I can rest in Your awesome acceptance and approval. I don't have to struggle to receive it. I only fight the good fight of faith because I love You. AMEN

Day Twelve

Morning

Positive Statement for the Day:

I Am A Unique Creation

Psalm 139:13-18

Oh yes, you shaped me first inside, then out;
you formed me in my mother's womb.
I thank you, High God—you're breathtaking!
Body and soul, I am marvelously made!
I worship in adoration—what a creation!
You know me inside and out,
you know every bone in my body;
You know exactly how I was made, bit by bit,
how I was sculpted from nothing into something.
Like an open book, you watched me grow from conception to
birth;
all the stages of my life were spread out before you,
The days of my life all prepared
before I'd even lived one day.
Your thoughts—how rare, how beautiful!
God, I'll never comprehend them!
I couldn't even begin to count them—
any more than I could count the sand of the sea.
Oh, let me rise in the morning and live always with you!

You are one of a kind! God made you with a unique combination of gifts, personality, and desires. No one else on the planet has the exact ingredients as you. The gifts, interests, talents, and experiences make you a unique creation. You are valuable and designed for a distinctive purpose.

Here is an important question, "Why spend so much time and energy trying to be like someone else?" If God had wanted you to be like them, He would have made you that way. You don't have the gifts another person has by design. Knowing what His purpose is for you, God gave you the gifts you need to fulfill it.

Your uniqueness makes you valuable. A one of a kind painting, car, or piece of furniture multiplies its value. The fact that you are distinct, irreplaceable, and unique makes you a valuable work of art in God's view and of vital importance in His kingdom.

Take time to both realize your uniqueness and to thank God for creating you as you are. Resist comparing yourself to another of God's creations. Embrace the fact that God, in His great design for all of humanity and His kingdom, has chosen to create you just as you are for an eternal purpose.

Open yourself up to the possibility that God actually knew what He was doing when He created you. Believe in His divine will and that you are an integral part of it.

Prayer Starter

I now know, Father, that You made me the way I am for a purpose. I regret all the time and energy I have wasted on wanting to be, and trying to be something other than what You created. I will appreciate my uniqueness. Thank You for my gifts, desires and personality. AMEN

"Check Up"

1. What are some of your unique gifts that cause you to stand apart from others?

_____

_____

2. Name some of the experiences from your life that have molded you into who you are now.

_____

_____

3. What topics or issues are you most passionate about in your life?

_____

_____

4. What observations did you make today while focusing on today's statement: I am a unique creation?

_____

_____

_____

_____

_____

_____

Prayer Starter

Lord, I have seen throughout this day that You created me unique for a purpose. I understand that You are wiser than I, and that You alone know the end from the beginning. You put me together in such a way as to make me the most effective for Your Kingdom. AMEN

Day Thirteen

Morning

Positive Statement for the Day:

I Have Royal Blood In My Bloodline

1 Peter 2:9-10

But you are the ones chosen by God,
chosen for the high calling of priestly work,
chosen to be a holy people,
God's instruments to do his work
and speak out for him,
to tell others of the night-and-day
difference he made for you—from nothing to something,
from rejected to accepted.

Nearly every child grows up with little royal fantasies in their play time. Little girls want to be the princess. They enjoy the dress up, the proper etiquette, and the hope for a dashing young prince on his white stead.

Little boys want to be the prince/knight. They want to slay the deadly, ferocious dragon. They want to defeat the enemy of the kingdom. They want to win and be the next in line to the throne.

I want to you to know, that in the realm of the Spirit of God that is not fantasy. According to His word, we are kings and priests. We have been adopted into the family of the King of kings and Lord of lords. He reigns over all the universe.

There is none like Him. No one can take His place on the throne. He is all powerful, all knowing and ever present. He is the "Lord Most High."

Now think for a moment. This great and mighty God we have described is your Father. You are a joint heir in the kingdom with Jesus Christ Himself.

You are not one of the little peons of the kingdom. You are not one of the slaves or sharecroppers. You are the chosen, royal priesthood of God Himself. He chose you for this position.

Isn't it time you begin to act like, walk like, and live like the royalty that you really are? You should hold your shoulders back and walk tall; you are the special, chosen, valuable, blessed, royal bloodline of God! You are part of a blood covenant. His blood is now applied to You.

The prodigal son had a brother, do you remember? His brother was living way below his privileges. Are you? Look at your life and see how you can act in a more royal fashion. I don't mean having the "royal wave," but the attitude that everything in the world is my Father's. You have unlimited access to your Dad, the King of the universe. Start acting like it today.

Prayer Starter

Dad, I'm so glad to be Your child. Thank You for adopting me into Your family. I want to live like the prince/princess that I now know I am because of You. I don't have to live below my privileges any longer. I will rise to the level You intended for me through the power of Your Spirit. Amen

"Check Up"

1. How did you fantasize during your childhood about being part of a royal family with a royal position?

_____

_____

2. Explain how being part of God's royal family could change your attitude.

_____

_____

3. Since you are an heir of God's kingdom, explain what that means.

_____

_____

4. What observations did you make today while focusing on today's statement: I have royal blood in my bloodline?

_____

_____

_____

_____

_____

_____

Prayer Starter

Father, Lord and King of the Universe, I thank You for adopting me into Your royal family. I am filled with gratitude that You have made me a part of Your kingly descendants. Help me live my life with that in mind. AMEN

Day Fourteen

Morning

Positive Statement for the Day:

My Past Is Forgiven And Erased, I'm A New Creation

2 Corinthians 5:17

Now we look inside, and what we see is that anyone united with the Messiah gets a fresh start, is created new. The old life is gone; a new life burgeons! Look at it!.

Galatians 2:20

Indeed, I have been crucified with Christ.
My ego is no longer central.
It is no longer important that I appear righteous before you or have your good opinion, and I am no longer driven to impress God. Christ lives in me.
The life you see me living is not "mine," but it is lived by faith in the Son of God, who loved me and gave himself for me. I am not going to go back on that.

Everyone has a past. Most people have things in their past that they are not proud of, or maybe are ashamed of. If only we could get past those previous sins and mistakes, perhaps we would feel free and able to experience the blessings God has for us.

Good news! God says in His word that ALL of your past is forgiven. It is erased. He does not remember it against you. You are cleansed in His sight. He has given you a new start. You get a clean slate in His eyes to begin again. He remembers our past against us NO MORE. Not even a little bit. He doesn't hold back some forgiveness to hold it over our heads so we will do right.

You are called a new creation. Old things have passed away (been forgiven and forgotten by God) and all things are now new. You get a "do over," a "mulligan," another chance with a clean sheet of paper to write the story of your life. In the spiritual world, you are a new person. Not a reconditioned you. Not a refinished version of the old you. You are not the Goodwill version, or the second hand edition, or even a new variety of the old. You are a brand new you in the paradigm of God.

See yourself as an original creation of God. He is the Creator. He alone can forgive and wipe away the past. His power is not limited. Starting over is not beyond His control or ability.

Your potential is even greater and vaster than your finite mind can comprehend. He has infused you with the power of His Holy Spirit to enable you to live a holy and righteous life with your new, clean sheet of paper as you write the fresh chapters of your new life.

Prayer Starter

Thank you Jesus for forgiving my past and erasing it. Help me erase it from my mind and to forgive myself. I realize now that I am a new creation. All that old stuff is dead and buried. I will now write upon the new page of my life with Your help. Assist me, Father, through Your Holy Spirit, to write upon it a holy, pure and purposeful ending to my new life's story. AMEN

"Check Up"

1. Write down what specific things God has forgiven you for.

_____

_____

2. How have you lived your new life since the old has been forgotten?

_____

_____

3. Explain how you have written the best on your new blank sheet of paper.

_____

_____

4. What observations did you make today while focusing on today's statement: My past is forgiven and erased, I'm a new creation.?

_____

_____

_____

_____

_____

_____

Prayer Starter

I am excited, Father, at the thought of writing a new story for my life with Your help. I am anticipating each day as we work together of create a legacy that is beyond my mistakes, failures and sins of the past. Thank You, Lord, for this great gift. AMEN

Day Fifteen

Morning

Positive Statement for the Day:

I Am Valuable And Blessed

Psalm 17:6-9

I call to you, God, because I'm sure of an answer.
So—answer! bend your ear! listen sharp!
Paint grace-graffiti on the fences;
take in your frightened children who
Are running from the neighborhood bullies
straight to you.
Keep your eye on me;
hide me under your cool wing feathers
From the wicked who are out to get me,
from mortal enemies closing in.

You are the apple of God's eye. He thinks that you are so valuable that He was willing to give His one and only Son, Jesus Christ to secure you. Just like you, God protects His valuables. He places you in His special place and wants to keep the "thief" away from you.

Since you are so valuable to Him, He is ready to bless you. He does not plan for you to just barely make it through life. His desire is that you trust Him and let Him pour out His blessings on you. You just have to learn how to access those blessings.

God has already given you everything that pertains to life and godliness. Too often we miss the first part: everything that pertains to life. God is not stingy. God is not a miser. God is extravagant and desires for you to be blessed so that you can be a blessing to those around you. To encourage yourself that the blessings of God are promised to you, read through Deuteronomy 28:1-14.

Some may have you to believe that we are all promised to be millionaires. That is hard to truthfully defend with a careful reading and study of God's word. But I believe that many Christians are living far below their promised privileges. God promises to meet our needs and to use us at some level to further the Gospel.

Let me encourage you to not focus on your lack. Don't mope about what you don't have, rather thank God for what you do have. Focus on what you can do with what God has already done for you. You are blessed to be a blessing. That is not always in a financial realm. You can bless others in many others ways.

Your value is not tied to your wealth or possessions. That value is intrinsic to your relationship with Almighty God, your awesome Creator. He values you. He holds you in high esteem. He believes in you. He wants to work with you to develop your opportunities. You are blessed and considered valuable because of Him

Prayer Starter
Father, I am so grateful that You see me as a person of value. I want to live my life in such a way as to receive the blessings You have for me, so that I can bless others. Thank You for helping me see what You think of me through Jesus Christ. AMEN

"Check Up"

1. How have you thought about God in the past? Is He ready and willing to bless you, or a stingy miser?

_____

_____

2. How have you received or sought validation that you are valuable outside of God and His word?

_____

_____

3. Other than financially, in what ways do you consider yourself blessed?

_____

_____

4. What observations did you make today while focusing on today's statement: I am valuable and blessed?

_____

_____

_____

_____

_____

_____

_____

Prayer Starter

What a day, Lord. Today I have realized and even felt at times how valuable and blessed I am because of You. You are the source of both my blessings and my sense of value. Thank You, Lord. AMEN

Section 4

MOTIVATED
By Faith

Day Sixteen

Morning

Positive Statement for the Day:

God Is Working All Things For My Good Today

Romans 8:18, 24, 25, 28

That's why I don't think there's any comparison between the present hard times and the coming good times.
The created world itself can hardly wait for what's coming next.
That is why waiting does not diminish us,
any more than waiting diminishes a pregnant mother.
We are enlarged in the waiting.
We, of course, don't see what is enlarging us.
But the longer we wait, the larger we become,
and the more joyful our expectancy.
That's why we can be so sure that every detail in our lives of love for God is worked into something good.

Have you ever taken the time to put one of those large jigsaw puzzles together? They can really be challenging. Once you begin to get the outer edge in place, you can see the possibilities of completing the puzzle. You begin to sort all the colors that go together and work on a section at a time. Maybe you focus on an object like a tree or a person and try to find all the pieces that look like they belong to that object and start putting that area together. It begins to take on real shape.

Still, sometimes all the different colors and shapes

seem to all blend together. Then you may just have to leave the table and come back later with a new, fresh look in order to make sense of the pieces.

That's what you are doing today! Your life can be considered a puzzle. There are many pieces to it. You wear many hats. You've experienced many things. Some of the pieces were from your life BC (before Christ) and other pieces are since you've become a Christian. Yet they all can, and will, fit together and make one beautiful masterpiece. Some of what you have experienced in your life has been difficult or hard to go through. Other parts have been easy and rewarding.

Today, God wants to show you that He is working all the pieces together. He is using all of the past events of your life to create a beautiful mastery piece out of them. The strength that you have developed through your past experiences is not wasted, but rather used to create an awesome section of your life's puzzle. So it is with the traits of perseverance, love, faith, hope, joy, or patience.

Today you will be focusing of the big picture. Take time to see how God has woven the pieces together to bring you to the good place you are today.

Prayer Starter
Lord, thanks for giving me a new perspective on my life. I appreciate it now more than ever. You are able to take all the pieces of my life and put them together in an awesome and beautiful fashion. Help me remember that today. AMEN

<u>"Check Up"</u>

1. What past events (good or bad) have made a lasting impact on your life?

    _____

    _____

2. How have those events formed you into the person you are today?

    _____

    _____

3. How can God use those events in your service as an ambassador for Him?

    _____

    _____

4. What observations did you make today while focusing on today's statement: God is working all things for my good today?

    _____

    _____

    _____

    _____

Prayer Starter

I love watching Your creative power, God. You are making something good out of all my life's experiences. I can see the puzzle coming together. Thank You for working all things together for my good. AMEN

Day Seventeen

Morning

Positive Statement for the Day:

Today, Everything Is Possible With God

Luke 1:37
Nothing, you see, is impossible with God.

Matthew 19:26
Jesus looked hard at them and said, "No chance at all if you think you can pull it off yourself. Every chance in the world if you trust God to do it."

Mark 9:23
Jesus said, "If? There are no 'ifs' among believers. Anything can happen."

What does your day look like? Is it filled with problems? Are you tempted to worry about situations and events that will possibly take place? Do you cry out in your spirit for a miracle from God to make it through the day? Are you bound by a spirit of fear over the unknown? Are you "under the circumstances" of your life and think there is now way out?

Well the word for the day should be an encouragement for you. You are reminded today that everything, no matter what, is possible with God. He is not limited to your thinking. He sees the end from the beginning. His hands are not tied by your circumstances. He is not fretting, worried, or caught by surprise as you face this day.

He has a totally different view of your circumstances. He has an elevated vision of everything going on in your life. He sees the totality of your life and knows that this present time is only a little fraction of the big picture for you.

He loves you. He desires to intervene in your life. Your total surrender to Him places His word and reputation on taking care of you. You are His special child. He is able and willing to show His great power through you.

All things are possible with your Heavenly Father. Nothing is too big for Him. He loves to show Himself strong on behalf of His children. You are in a great place for the miracle hand of Almighty God to prove His great love and care for you today. Expect Him to take over and do what you think is impossible.

An old gospel song recites, "He specializes in things thought impossible." Believe that. Cling to that. Keep that phrase in your mind as you push through your life today. Together, you and God will make it to the other side of the problems. You do your part (surrender) and He will do His part (the impossible).

Prayer Starter

Heavenly Father, today is going to be great as I live for You. I trust You to move in the areas of my life that I think are impossible. I praise You in faith that You are going to do the miraculous and take care of me today. AMEN.

"Check Up"

1. What has been overwhelming you to the point of fear and hopelessness?

   _____

   _____

2. How have you tried to take care of these matters before surrendering them to God?

   _____

   _____

3. What steps have you taken to totally surrender your concerns to your loving Heavenly Father?

   _____

   _____

4. What observations did you make today while focusing on today's statement: Today, everything is possible with God?

   _____

   _____

   _____

   _____

   _____

   _____

Prayer Starter

I trust you, Father. I know that You have both the power and inclination to work on my behalf. Thank you for helping me surrender throughout this day so that I can see Your mighty hand do the impossible for me. AMEN

Day Eighteen

Morning

Positive Statement for the Day:

Today, I Walk In The Blessing Of God

Proverbs 10:22
God's blessing makes life rich;
nothing we do can improve on God.

Psalm 1:3
You're a tree replanted in Eden,
bearing fresh fruit every month,
Never dropping a leaf,
always in blossom.

Psalm 35:27
But those who want
the best for me,
Let them have the last word—a glad shout!—
and say, over and over and over,
"GOD is great—everything works
together for good for his servant."

This is your day! Today you are going to continually remind yourself that God is in the blessing business. He is going to work things in your favor. You will be amazed as you remember how much your Father in Heaven is ready to pour out His incredible blessings on your life.

Focus on the possibilities today, not the problems. Center your thoughts on His promise of blessing, not on the world's preoccupation with lack and poverty. Concentrate today on the many promises of your Father to make you the object of His approval and esteem.

Open your eyes today, and see with a fresh awareness, that God wants to bless you. Look for the ways that He is working. Watch as He puts profitable things in your path. Listen to His voice as He guides you to make decisions that are filled with promise and possibility. Be aware of the doors of opportunity He will place before you.

Refuse to allow an attitude of complacency toward your current situation. Remember you have been justified, sanctified and set apart. The just live by faith, not by sight.

Your faith is in God Almighty. Jehovah Jireh. He wants to pour out His blessings on you. Not so that you can consume it on yourself, but so that your needs are met and you have the ability to be a blessing for His Kingdom.

Reject the thoughts that place God contrary to His word. He has stated His inclination, His desire, and His plan to bless you. Don't accept anything less than the blessing of God on your life. Decree it. Declare it. Believe it. You walk in the blessing of God.

Prayer Starter

God, You are truly an awesome Father. Thank You for Your desire to bless me as Your child. You are thrilled to give to me. It warms Your heart. I will look everywhere today for the blessing You have promised me. AMEN

"Check Up"

1. In what ways have you allowed yourself to accept that God does not want to bless you?

_____

_____

2. How has God met your financial and business needs in the past?

_____

_____

3. How have you been faithful to be a blessing to God's Kingdom when you were blessed in the past?

_____

_____

4. What observations did you make today while focusing on today's statement: Today, I walk in the blessing of God?

_____

_____

_____

_____

_____

_____

Prayer Starter

I am in awe of You, God. You have helped me see how much You desire to bless me. Now I understand that Your great love for me includes the fact that You desire to bless me as Your child. AMEN

Day Nineteen

Morning

Positive Statement for the Day:

I Can Do All Things Through Jesus Today

Philippians 4:10-13

*I'm glad in God, far happier than you would ever guess—
happy that you're again showing such strong concern for me.
Not that you ever quit praying and thinking about me. You just
had no chance to show it. Actually, I don't have a sense of
needing anything personally. I've learned by now to be quite
content whatever my circumstances. I'm just as happy with
little as with much, with much as with little. I've found the
recipe for being happy whether full or hungry, hands full or
hands empty. Whatever I have, wherever I am, I can make it
through anything in the One who makes me who I am.*

Most of us realize that Jesus can do anything. He is
part of the Godhead and has the glory and power associated
with that position. Nothing is too hard for Him. He is the
Word (Logos) that was involved in the creation of all things
(John 1).

In Genesis 18, God renews His promise to Abraham
regarding a son. This time He set a date that Sarah would give
birth in nine months. Sarah laughs. God hears her and makes
this statement in verse 14, "Is anything too hard for the
LORD?"

God is all powerful, all knowing, all seeing, and ever present. He is able to speak and it comes to pass. Jesus is proof of the power and love of God toward you.

Even though Jesus is able in this day and age (the church age), His decision is to NOT do all things. Instead, He empowered the church with His Holy Spirit so they (the church) can do all things through Him and for Him.

You are part of the church. His Spirit resides within you and will empower to do all things. Your faith is the catalyst by which the Holy Spirit of God is activated in your life and in your situations.

The program of God is to build His kingdom by possessing you with His Spirit and you doing the works. That's why He says you can do all things through Christ, Who strengthens you.

What kind of things? All things! Personal problems and challenges, business trials and tribulations, ministry opportunities and visions all fall under the umbrella of "all things." You can do it with help from Jesus through His Spirit. John actually calls the Holy Spirit your Helper. He will empower, encourage and escort you through the processes needed to accomplish God's will. You are never alone.

Prayer Starter

Father God, thank You for choosing to work through me. Today I will walk in faith that I may activate Your Spirit who lives in me. Together we will advance and build Your kingdom. My life is Yours, oh God. AMEN

"Check Up"

1. What do you have to do today that you will rely on Jesus and His Spirit to accomplish?

_____

_____

2. Have you allowed the Holy Spirit to become your Helper so that you can do all things through Christ?

_____

_____

3. How are you willing to include "all things," even the small stuff, in your reliance for help from Jesus?

_____

_____

4. What observations did you make today while focusing on today's statement: I can do all things through Jesus today?

_____

_____

_____

_____

_____

_____

Prayer Starter

Thank You, Lord for helping me do everything today. I could feel your strong arms around me as I undertook each task before me. You helped me. Your Spirit guided me. I did it. We did it together. AMEN

Day Twenty

Morning

Positive Statement for the Day:

I Will Move From Believing To Expecting

Psalm 62:5-8

God, the one and only—
I'll wait as long as he says.
Everything I hope for comes from him,
so why not?
He's solid rock under my feet,
breathing room for my soul,
An impregnable castle:
I'm set for life.
My help and glory are in God
—granite-strength and safe-harbor-God—
So trust him absolutely, people;
lay your lives on the line for him.
God is a safe place to be.

Salvation is by faith and by faith alone. Not of works so that none of us can boast about what we have done.

The Bible is also clear that we are to live by faith. Most of us have heard, "Seeing is believing." But the inverse is also true, "Believing is seeing."

Believing is central to the Christian message and the life of the believer. Most of the message of the Bible is that we must believe. Believe God loves us. Believe Jesus is His Son. Believe Jesus died and rose from the dead. Believe Jesus is coming back. On and on we are told to believe. We are told in Hebrews 11 that without faith, it is impossible to please God.

We are also told that we should expect God to respond to our faith. We should be a Church of His children (called and anointed by God) that expects our Father to show up, to bless us, to protect us, and to never leave us. What are you expecting from God? Not just a generic hope, but real expectation. Look at your life and the ways in which God has helped you in the past. He has not changed.

When you go to church, do you just hope something will happen? Maybe you even doubt that anything significant will take place. Why not begin expecting that God will show up. Why not anticipate His glory being revealed and lives being changed? According to 2 Peter 1:4, God has "… given us exceedingly great and precious promises." Why not look forward to their fulfillment with intense expectation?

When we ask through prayer, we should believe and expect that our loving Heavenly Father is going to move on our behalf. He will not leave us hanging.

Prayer Starter
Dearest Lord, I know that I often run to You and present my requests during our time together. I'm sorry for just compiling a list of wants or complaints. Build in me a sense of expectation that You can, will, and want to respond to my prayers. AMEN

"Check Up"

1. How do you think having a spirit of expectation will affect your life?

_____

_____

2. What things have dampened your expectation that God is willing to move in your life?

_____

_____

3. What specific things are you expecting God to do in your life this week?

_____

_____

4. What observations did you make today while focusing on today's statement: I will move from believing to expecting?

_____

_____

_____

_____

_____

Prayer Starter

It works, Father! It really works! When I, in faith, expect You to fulfill Your great and precious promises, You do it! I know it's not some magical word or trick. It's just that I am aligning myself with Your will and as my Heavenly Father, You delight in responding to my faith and expectation. This is going to change my life. AMEN

Section 5

MOTIVATED
By Doing God's Will

Day Twenty One

Morning

Positive Statement for the Day:

I Am Full Of Potential

2 Peter 1:2-4

Grace and peace to you many times over as you deepen in your experience with God and Jesus, our Master.

Don't Put It Off

Everything that goes into a life of pleasing God has been miraculously given to us by getting to know, personally and intimately, the One who invited us to God. The best invitation we ever received!
We were also given absolutely terrific promises to pass on to you—your tickets to participation in the life of God after you turned your back on a world corrupted by lust.

You are full of potential! That's right you. There are possibilities all around you and you have the right mix of personality, gifts, experiences, and passions to rise to greatness through the anointing of the Spirit of God.

Sadly, most of us have never risen to even half of the potential that God has placed in us. We have allowed negative thoughts and actions to diminish our worthiness. We have become enslaved by our past rather than understanding we are free from it through the blood of Jesus. If we will actually learn from our previous actions (or lack of the same) we can overcome and use those things in our life as we minister to others. We can empathize with people because of what we have been through. Yet, we have spoken negatively to ourselves and not built upon our strengths.

God's plan for you involves developing the possibilities that lie dormant in and around you. There are so many things within you that, if focused on and developed, would make you into a mighty child of God.

You don't have to look for something else to be used effectively by Jesus. Just allow Him to develop what He has already given you. You can discover the concealed, suppressed, latent possibilities within you. You can tap into that potential.

Out of your spirit can flow an artesian well of creativity. You have undiscovered, even camouflaged, capabilities that will propel you into God's destiny for your life.

The key here is surrender to Him. Understand the potential He placed in and around you is part of His perfect plan for your life. I've often heard it said, "God doesn't need your ability, but your availability."

Prayer Starter

Father God, thank You for filling my life with unbelievable potential. Help me realize that it is lying dormant in my life and give me the wisdom and power I need to use that potential to serve You. AMEN

"Check Up"

1. What potential do you honestly feel in your spirit was placed there by God?

_____

_____

2. How can you unearth this potential and use it effectively for the Kingdom of God?

_____

_____

3. What changes must you make to your life in order to develop the potential within you?

_____

_____

4. What observations did you make today while focusing on today's statement: I am full of potential?

_____

_____

_____

_____

_____

_____

Prayer Starter

Lord, I have seen the latent potential in my life today. Thank You for opening my eyes and showing me what is possible with my life. I need Your help and power to develop the potential You have given me. Show me the opportunities I need to follow to cultivate them. AMEN

Day Twenty Two

Morning

Positive Statement for the Day:

I Will Not Settle For Mediocrity

Jeremiah 29:11-13

I know what I'm doing.
I have it all planned out—plans to take care of you,
not abandon you, plans to give you the future you hope for.
"When you call on me, when you come and pray to me,
I'll listen
."When you come looking for me, you'll find me.
"Yes, when you get serious about finding me and want it more
than anything else,
I'll make sure you won't be disappointed."

You were created, gifted, and empowered for more than a mediocre life! Just getting by and making little difference in the Kingdom of God is not how He made you. Deep within you is a seed of greatness. You have dreams and desires that go way beyond the reality you are living every day.

Why have you allowed an attitude of just getting by and barely making it to rule your thoughts? Why have you stopped pushing for excellence and becoming a dynamic force in God's Kingdom? What events have pushed your optimism to the grave? Who has told you that you are just average and to not expect greatness from anything you try?

I'm sure you have had obstacles like everyone else. You've probably been knocked down more than once. Maybe life hasn't always served you well. Maybe all your opportunities have not all given you what you thought they would.

Have you permitted a thought process of mediocrity to creep in? Just because your obstacles and problems require more work or another try doesn't have to mean that you settle.

God created you for excellence. He did not design you to be an average, middle-of-the-road, run of the mill, common place person.

He creates things that are good, actually, very good (see Genesis 1). He made you to be exceptional.

The bottom line is, if you are settling with a mediocre life, it is because you made the decision to do so. Your decisions and habits have formed you into who you are today.

Good News! You can change that decision today and form the attitude within you to not allow yourself to become content, satisfied or at ease with a mediocre life.

Prayer Starter

I confess my mediocrity to You, Jesus. I have gotten lazy and been satisfied with less than Your best. With Your help and power I will banish mediocrity from my life. I resolve to live the exceptional life You intended for me to live. AMEN

"Check Up"

1. In what areas of your life have you settled for mediocrity?

   _____

   _____

2. What caused you to stop expecting excellence and start being content with average?

   _____

   _____

3. How do you think your decision to not settle for less than God's best will affect you now?

   _____

   _____

4. What observations did you make today while focusing on today's statement: I will not settle for mediocrity?

   _____

   _____

   _____

   _____

   _____

   _____

Prayer Starter

I could see it today, Lord. My eyes were definitely opened to how I have surrendered to areas of mediocrity instead of pushing and believing for Your best. I now see You as a God of excellence. With Your help, strength and power I will no longer make excuses for my average thoughts. AMEN

Day Twenty Three

Morning

Positive Statement for the Day:

I Will Follow My Dream

Psalm 37:3-8
Get insurance with GOD and do a good deed,
settle down and stick to your last.
Keep company with GOD,
get in on the best.
Open up before GOD, keep nothing back;
he'll do whatever needs to be done:
He'll validate your life in the clear light of day
and stamp you with approval at high noon.
Quiet down before GOD,
be prayerful before him.
Don't bother with those who climb the ladder,
who elbow their way to the top.
Bridle your anger, trash your wrath,
cool your pipes—it only makes things worse

You have a dream! Yes, you do. You may have submerged it into your subconscious, but you have a dream. Maybe you've allowed the "reality" of life to sterilize your dream, but you have one somewhere deep within you.

Sometimes we have allowed the necessities of our daily activities to snuff out the flame of our dream. We have buried the possibilities that lie within us and placed a R.I.P. sign as its marker.

Well, it's time for a miracle.   It's time for a resurrection.   It's time to allow the Spirit of God to breathe new life into that old dream and to make it come to pass.

If you will trust in God and delight yourself also in Him, He will give you the desires of your heart.   Your dream. Your goals, visions and aspirations.

Joseph had dreams.   As a young boy he dreamed of the way God would use him and even raise him up above his brothers.   Those dreams were pushed down for decades. Joseph endured hardship and testing during that time.

Then God stirred them up and open the door for the magnificent fulfillment of Joseph's comatose dreams and they became reality.   Joseph sat as Prime Minister over all of Egypt and eventually his brothers knelt before him.

Your dream can still happen.   You are not dead yet. You have not exhausted all of your options.   Your life is not spent.   You can take the necessary steps to begin to fulfill your heart's desire.

God gave you the dream, and He is not finished with you yet.   You don't have to grieve over a dead dream any longer.   Start now to pursue it.

Prayer Starter
Lord, thank You for my dream.   Help me resurrect it. Give a fresh passion for it.   Show me Your plan for its fulfillment.   Give me the strength to make it happen.   AMEN

"Check Up"

1. What dreams have you allowed to be put on the back burner of your life?

_____

_____

2. What has happened to those dreams? What caused you to stop pursuing them?

_____

_____

3. God implanted the dream within you. How can you resurrect that dream?

_____

_____

4. What observations did you make today while focusing on today's statement: I will follow my dream?

_____

_____

_____

_____

_____

_____

Prayer Starter

Thank You, Lord, for renewing my passion for the dreams You have given me. I praise You that You are faithful to prod me to fulfill Your will. I have made the choice to step out in faith and focus on the big picture. I will trust You and delight in You. As Your word promises, You will then give me the desires of my heart. AMEN

Day Twenty Four

Morning

Positive Statement for the Day:

God Puts The Extra In My Ordinary

Ephesians 3:20-21
God can do anything, you know—
far more than you could ever imagine or guess or request in
your wildest dreams!
He does it not by pushing us around
but by working within us,
his Spirit deeply and gently within us.
Glory to God in the church!
Glory to God in the Messiah, in Jesus!
Glory down all the generations!
Glory through all millennia! Oh, yes!

You don't have to face life and its challenges in your own strength. You will wear yourself out if the only resources you use are your own power, your own thoughts, and your own plans. Going it alone, will cause burn out or a loss of effectiveness.

Too many people have found out that they don't have what it takes. History is full of people who tried to follow God in their own strength. They thought if they just fought harder, resisted louder, gave more, or denied themselves, then they could overcome and be able to stand before God victorious.

Does that describe you?

If you are going to rely in any of your works, let it be this, if you will put forth effort, even in your own strength, and submit the outcome to Almighty God, He will add the extra to your ordinary and make the results extra-ordinary.

Just imagine an ordinary bottle of water. It is good and good for you. But if you pour in a packet of energy powder (I prefer the cherry flavored), the ordinary water changes. It's still good and good for you, but now it tastes better and gives you EXTRA energy to help you through the day.

God's power (powder) is in the Holy Spirit that He adds to your ordinary actions. He can raise your effectiveness and create a dynamic life for you each day.

Jesus made it clear in John 15 that without Him, you can do nothing. But He goes on to say that if you abide in Him and His words abide in you, then you can ask what you desire and it will be done for you.

He will do the exceeding, abundant, over the top of everything that you ask or think. He does it according to the power that is working in you. He puts the extra in your ordinary.

Prayer Starter
I realize, Heavenly Father, that You are the missing ingredient to my ordinary actions. You are able and willing to add Your power to my actions to create the extra-ordinary in and through me. I submit to Your additive of the Holy Spirit today. AMEN

"Check Up"

1. What area of your life or walk with God are you trying to accomplish in your own strength?

   _____

   _____

2. How can you surrender those areas in order to have them infused with the power of God?

   _____

   _____

3. How is the power of God at work in your life? He says He'll add to it according the power working in you.

   _____

   _____

4. What observations did you make today while focusing on today's statement: God puts the extra in my ordinary?

   _____

   _____

   _____

   _____

   _____

   _____

Prayer Starter

I realize, Heavenly Father, that You are extraordinary! Everything You do is great. You have worked awesomely in my life. Just as You took the little boy's lunch and fed thousands, so You promise to take my ordinary actions and create amazing results. AMEN

Day Twenty Five

Morning

Positive Statement for the Day:

Today I Will Walk In Victory

Romans 8:31-39

So, what do you think? With God on our side like this, how can we lose? If God didn't hesitate to put everything on the line for us, embracing our condition and exposing himself to the worst by sending his own Son, is there anything else he wouldn't gladly and freely do for us? And who would dare tangle with God by messing with one of God's chosen? Who would dare even to point a finger? The One who died for us— who was raised to life for us!—is in the presence of God at this very moment sticking up for us. Do you think anyone is going to be able to drive a wedge between us and Christ's love for us? There is no way! Not trouble, not hard times, not hatred, not hunger, not homelessness, not bullying threats, not backstabbing, not even the worst sins listed in Scripture: They kill us in cold blood because they hate you.   We're sitting ducks; they pick us off one by one.

None of this fazes us because Jesus loves us. I'm absolutely convinced that nothing—nothing living or dead, angelic or demonic, today or tomorrow, high or low, thinkable or unthinkable—absolutely nothing can get between us and God's love because of the way that Jesus our Master has embraced us.

Your mindset often determines your outcome. When you realize that you can do something, and begin in faith to speak that through the Spirit, you open the door of victory in your life.

You do not have to sin today. It's not necessary for you to have a bad attitude today. You don't have to use bad language today. It is possible and preferable that you learn to flee from sin and to walk in holiness.

It's not easy, but it is attainable. God has already given you the power to stand against the schemes of Satan. He has given you the armor of God to prepare you for the battle.

Of all the great things that Jesus did during His earthly time, perhaps the greatest statement about Him is that He didn't sin. Although tempted, He never gave in. Jesus expects us to strive for this.

You can make up your mind today to walk in total victory through this battle field. You can end the day pure and holy before God singing,

> "Victory is mine, victory is mine
> Victory today is Mine.
> I told old Satan, get thee behind.
> Victory today is mine."

Prayer Starter
Almighty Father, I pray for Your help this day. I want to walk in holiness and purity. I desire to not let sin dictate and control my life. I put my foot down and say that I will be victorious this day. Thank You for Your help and power to help me succeed. AMEN

"Check Up"

1. In which areas of your life have you been experiencing defeat on a regular basis?

   _____

   _____

2. What one thing can you do on a daily basis that would help you walk in victory in the above areas?

   _____

   _____

3. If you believe that God intends for you to walk in victory, how can He help you make it a reality?

   _____

   _____

4. What observations did you make today while focusing on today's statement: Today I will walk in victory?

   _____

   _____

   _____

   _____

   _____

   _____

Prayer Starter

Thank You, God for the victory I experienced today. I realize that every little victory will build until I have totally overcome in the areas of my weakness. Thank You for Your power that helps me be strong so that the victory You have promised is attainable. AMEN

Section 6

MOTIVATED
By A Purpose

Day Twenty Six

Morning

Positive Statement for the Day:

I Have Everything I Need To Fulfill My Destiny

2 Peter 1:2-4

Grace and peace to you many times over as you deepen in your experience with God and Jesus, our Master.
Don't Put It Off
[3-4]*Everything that goes into a life of pleasing God has been miraculously given to us by getting to know, personally and intimately, the One who invited us to God. The best invitation we ever received! We were also given absolutely terrific promises to pass on to you—your tickets to participation in the life of God after you turned your back on a world corrupted by lust.*

God has a plan for your life! He allowed you to experience each situation and circumstance so that you could fulfill your destiny. Even the things that are, or have been hard, hurtful or even painful, God is able to use them to make you into the vessel of choice that will produce the best for your life and make a real difference in others.

You have been given gifts both in the natural and in the spiritual realm. 1 Peter 4:10 confirms that fact.

Your personal talents and abilities are gifts from God,

as well as those listed in the Scriptures (Romans 12:3-8, 1 Corinthians 12, and Ephesians 4:7-16). Even your personal desires and dreams are part of God's gifting and provision for you. He placed them in your spirit as well.

God is a planner. When He created everything, He did it according the plan in His mind. Things were created in a specific order that was necessary for a good result. He couldn't very well create the trees without some dry ground to place them in or a sun to shine on them. He is the consummate planner.

The Bible is a record of His plan for the human race. Beyond the historical data of people, times, and events, we see His mighty and perfect plan coming together. He planned the lineage through which the Messiah would eventually come. When the time was right He sent Jesus. When the time is right, He will send Him again. There is a perfect plan for the fruition of all things.

He planned for you. You are not an accident! God planned your destiny in such detail, that you already have everything you need to fulfill His plan for your life. This is an awesome thought. You have been endowed with exactly what you need to accomplish your purpose in life.

In order to realize the fullness of that statement, you just have to surrender your heart and life to Him. He is ready to walk you through the plan He has for you. You will be more fulfilled, content and satisfied as you uncover His design for you.

Prayer Starter

Father, I praise You that I can trust You with my entire life! I surrender my destiny to You right now. Thank you for giving me everything I need to fulfill Your plan for my life. AMEN

"Check Up"

1. How can you see God's plan at work in your life?

_____

_____

_____

2. What gifts, both natural and spiritual, have you discovered that God has given you to fulfill His divine purpose?

_____

_____

_____

3. How has God developed and used those gifts He placed within you?

_____

_____

_____

4. What observations did you make today while focusing on today's statement: I have everything I need to fulfill my destiny?

_____

_____

_____

_____

_____

_____

_____

Prayer Starter

Lord, thank You for opening my eyes today to see that You have given me all that I need to fulfill Your plan for my life. Help me guide others to see this truth as well. AMEN.

Day Twenty Seven

Morning

Positive Statement for the Day:

I Know God Has Good Things In Store For Me

Psalm 34:8-10
*Open your mouth and taste, open your eyes and see—
how good GOD is.
Blessed are you who run to him.*

*Worship GOD if you want the best;
worship opens doors to all his goodness.*

*Young lions on the prowl get hungry,
but GOD-seekers are full of God.*

Have you ever heard someone going through a tough time say something like, "Why does God have it in for me? Why is He sending this my way?"

A lot of people have the idea that if they are not perfect, God is like some kind of heavenly bully wanting to hurt them.   It's as if they feel like they deserve some punishment for their actions and they blame God for it.

Listen very carefully to me. If you are a child of God remember this well. God has good things in store for you. He is thinking about you and the Bible says He thinks thoughts of peace and not of evil, to give you a future and a hope.

Don't listen to any other voice in your head, or outside your head. God is a good God. He loves His children. Don't ascribe to God the work of Satan, the world, or your own flesh.

The psalmist repeatedly confess that the LORD is good and His mercy endures forever. Praise the name of the LORD.

God wants the best for you. His thoughts and plans are for your good, not bad. Trust Him in this.

Not everything in life is simple. Not every person is easy to get along with. Some situations are awful. Some jobs just flat out stink. Regardless of other people, situations or jobs, you can always rest in the fact that your Heavenly Father is good, and will always be good to you.

Marinate on that thought all day. See how He has blessed you in the smallest areas of your life. Things that perhaps we take for granted on a daily basis.

Begin to praise Him for those things and people. Even the small things. Cultivate an attitude of praise and thanksgiving for the great goodness of God. What we preachers like to call an, "Attitude of Gratitude."

Prayer Starter
Father, I praise You for Your goodness. Even though I may feel like I'm not worthy of it, Your attitude toward me is good. Help me remember that today. Help me grow in that thought all day. AMEN

"Check Up"

1. Have you ever blamed God for "having it out for you?
   Write those instances here.

   _____

   _____

2. How has the truth that God has good things in store for you
   changed your attitude?

   _____

   _____

3. Can you see now that some people can be used by God to
   create the good He promised for you? Who?

   _____

   _____

4. What observations did you make today while focusing on
   today's statement: I know God has good things in store
   for me?

   _____

   _____

   _____

   _____

   _____

   _____

   _____

Prayer Starter
*Thank You, Lord! I have seen Your goodness all
around me today. You indeed are good and Your mercy
endures forever. Blessed be the name of the Lord. AMEN*

Day Twenty Eight

Morning

Positive Statement for the Day:

I Have A
Bright Future

Jeremiah 29:11-13
I know what I'm doing.
I have it all planned out—plans to take care of you,
not abandon you, plans to give you the future you hope for.

"When you call on me, when you come and pray to me, I'll
listen. "When you come looking for me, you'll find me.

"Yes, when you get serious about finding me and want it more
than anything else, I'll make sure you won't be disappointed."

Do you ever wonder what the future holds? There are billions of dollars spent each year on palm readings, astrology, and mediums as people want to know something, anything, about their future. Many movies have been made where people can tell or sense the future.

The word of God gives a lot of information about the future. It may not give you exact details on the name, date and color of hair concerning who you are going to marry, but it does give you the main things. Mostly, if you are living for God, the Bible lets you know that your future is bright. God looks out for His children and provides for and protects them.

Following Him and His word gives you peace and security. Listening to His voice gives you real direction so that your decisions are good and prosperous. Seeking Him and His will gives you joy. If you seek first the Kingdom of God and His righteousness, all other things will be added to you. This relates to a decisively good future. If you believe in God, and that He is One who keeps His word and promises, then even a quick reading of the Bible shows how God has distinctive, good futures designed for His followers. He makes promises and statements that give you strong reason to believe that He wants a good future for you. Even in the end, God has stated there is laid up for you a crown of righteousness and an eternal existence that is beyond anything you can imagine. No good thing has He withheld from those who love and obey Him.

Even if your past is checkered with all types of mistakes, failures and sins God has a good future designed for you. Release the past. Let go of your mistakes. Learn from your failures. Confess your sins. Now, look to God in faith and starting walking in and talking about the unrelenting goodness of your God. He has thoughts of good toward you and your future. Trust Him. Lean on Him. And watch Him bring it to reality in your life. Have hope in His promises and in His nature. He is not like a man who may lie. He is constant, truthful, and faithful. If He says it, which He does, He will be faithful to complete it in you.

Prayer Starter

God, I trust You. It's not always easy, but I know that You have a plan and a future for me that is bright and blessed. I surrender to Your will and I accept Your blessing today. AMEN

"Check Up"

1. What are some of the alternate ways you have tried to find out about your future?

_____

_____

2. No one ever dreams about a bad future. What dreams have you had about a bright future?

_____

_____

3. How are you cooperating with God and His will so that His bright future for you can actually happen?

_____

_____

4. What observations did you make today while focusing on today's statement: I have a bright future?

_____

_____

_____

_____

_____

_____

Prayer Starter

Thank You, Lord, for Your goodness toward me and for thinking good thoughts about me. Help me to continue to step into Your light and to seek Your kingdom. I want to know You better. I will rely on Your promises and statements that proclaim Your goodness. AMEN

Day Twenty Nine

Morning

Positive Statement for the Day:

> # My Best Days Are Ahead Of Me

Psalm 1:1-3
How well God must like you—
you don't hang out at Sin Saloon,
you don't slink along Dead-End Road,
you don't go to Smart-Mouth College.

Instead you thrill to GOD's Word,
you chew on Scripture day and night.
You're a tree replanted in Eden,
bearing fresh fruit every month,
Never dropping a leaf,
always in blossom.

Have you ever met someone who talks continually about how great the "good old days" were? They focus on some special time, event, or person in their past life. I'm pretty certain we have all met someone like that. You and I could easily become like that, for all of us have had some really good times in the past. We've all experienced joy, happiness, and spiritual fulfillment. Maybe the decisions we've made have dampened our happiness, or the way others have treated us has stomped on our joy. Even with the pressures of the world around us, we have allowed our walk with God to get powerless and routine.

But guess what? It doesn't have to be that way anymore. God has plans for you. Great plans. Awesome plans. You don't have to live in the glories of the past. Your best days are ahead of you. Don't view the past as just a limitation on your future. Don't let it determine your future days. Instead, let your past become an indicator of how God wants to work in your life today and tomorrow. The things that you have gone through, both the good and the bad, are just the perfect ingredients for God to use to create a powerful and effective future in your life.

God is not finished with you and your life! Don't accept the lie of the devil that wants you to believe that your best days are in the past. Rather, believe that God is always planning, ever designing, continually fulfilling His desire that you move from glory to glory and have better and brighter days as you continue to follow Him.

Your best days are going to be like a tree that is planted and unmovable. They are promised to be fruitful and not withering. Everything you do will prosper. It sounds like a great plan from God's word doesn't it? Have faith. Look forward. Anticipate the ways that your God will bless you. Cooperate in His design for you. Pray that His will be done in your life each day.

Prayer Starter

Father, thank You for helping me understand that You are in control. That You are going to make the rest of my life better than anything I've ever known. I am grateful for my past blessings, I understand now that they are just indicators of Your great plan for me now. AMEN.

"Check Up"

1. What are some of the best days you remember from your past?

   _____

   _____

2. What did you learn from the past about your greatest past achievements?

   _____

   _____

3. How can you cooperate with God and experience better days in the future?

   _____

   _____

4. What observations did you make today while focusing on today's statement: My best days are ahead of me?

   _____

   _____

   _____

   _____

   _____

   _____

Prayer Starter

Thank You, Lord, for Your goodness toward me and for thinking good thoughts about me. Help me to continue to step into Your light and to seek Your kingdom. I want to know You better. I will rely on Your promises and statements that proclaim Your goodness. AMEN

Day Thirty

Morning

Positive Statement for the Day:

I Will Not Limit God

Psalm 78:7-8

Know the truth and tell the stories
so their children can trust in God,
Never forget the works of God
but keep his commands to the letter.
Heaven forbid they should be like their parents,
bullheaded and bad,
A fickle and faithless bunch
who never stayed true to God.

Psalm 78:40-42

How often in the desert they had spurned him,
tried his patience in those wilderness years.
Time and again they pushed him to the limit,
provoked Israel's Holy God.
How quickly they forgot what he'd done,
forgot their day of rescue from the enemy,

When I first read this passage (verse 41) in the New King James Version years ago, it did a real number on my head, not to mention my theology. The almighty, all knowing, and ever present Creator of all that is was limited. Did it really say that? I had to read it several times before the truth came to me.

You read verses like, "With God all things are possible," and "Now unto Him Who is able to do exceedingly abundantly above all we can ask or think." began to rack my brain. How can God be limited?

Then God helped me. I realized that the limitation was not with God Himself, but with the attitude of the people. Verse 42 goes on to explain how they limited God's movement in their midst by saying that, "They did not remember His power."

Have you forgotten how God has shown Himself strong in your life? Have you stopped to think about where you would be today if it were not for His mighty hand working on your behalf? Have you allowed the miraculous ways of God to slip into the caverns of your forgetfulness? According to these scriptures, you limit God when you don't remember His powerful intervention in your past.

Your faith is being continually constructed. It is based on God's previous works in the word and in your life. Today you will recall the mighty acts of God. Think of how He moved in the Scriptures. Focus on how He has answered your prayers and intervened for you in the past. He is the same. He does not change. We can have faith for Him to move in our life by remembering what He has done.

Prayer Starter
Lord, I'm sorry for limiting Your work in my life. I will take the time today to remember what awesome things You have done for me, to me and with me in the past. Help me build my faith in Your desire to work in my life. AMEN.

"Check Up"

1. List the miraculous ways God has intervened in your past that you may have forgotten.

   _____

   _____

2. Why do you think you had forgotten how God moved in your past situations?

   _____

   _____

3. After reflecting on God's past work in your life, how can you have faith to believe Him for help now?

   _____

   _____

4. What observations did you make today while focusing on today's statement: I will not limit God?

   _____

   _____

   _____

   _____

   _____

   _____

Prayer Starter

Thank You, Father, for helping me remember. You have done some awesome things in my life. You promised to never leave me and to never forsake me. You have intervened in my life in miraculous ways. I can't help but to trust You now. I know that You will show Your great and mighty power on my behalf again. AMEN

Section 7

MOTIVATED
By An Attitude

Day Thirty One

Morning

Positive Statement for the Day:

God Is Thinking Good Thoughts About Me Today

Jeremiah 29:11
I know what I'm doing.
I have it all planned out—
plans to take care of you, not abandon you,
plans to give you the future you hope for.

There is a whole line of greeting cards devoted to "Thinking of You." Go into any card store or section and look at all the encouraging messages we can send to one another. There is something powerful that is conveyed when someone lets you know they are thinking about you. Just a little card that is mailed or handed to you can lift your spirits and remind you that you are not alone or without support.

Wouldn't it be a fantastic thing to realize that someone is thinking about you every day? Knowing that you are on the mind of another can give you comfort and strength to push through whatever you may face. Someone else believes in you. Someone else realizes that you are going through a difficult time and cared enough to let you know that they are behind you. They are pulling for you to get beyond it. They believe that you have what it takes to step up during these pressing times and come out victorious. It would be great to receive one of these types of cards every day, especially today.

Well, here it is. You are on God's mind today, and every day. He is thinking about you. He is focusing His vast intellect on His children, and that means you!

Remember that as your Heavenly Father is thinking about you, He is thinking good thoughts about you. It's not like He's scheming about ways to "get" you or to punish you. He loves you more than you can imagine. He is thinking good, nice, and wonderful thoughts about you. He is working an awesome plan for your life and He is putting real thought into how He can bless, protect, and provide for you.

One of the schemes of the devil has been to paint a picture of God as a hateful, destructive force. This has produced people who have an unfounded fear in a relationship with God. They see Him as judgmental. This worldview even creates a view that God loves to punish. But His word reveals Him as loving and merciful to His children.

Remember, you are the apple of His eye. He looks upon you with great love. He wants the best for you. You are not alone. You don't have to "go it alone."

God, your Father, is thinking good thoughts about you today and that should encourage you. It should lift your spirits. It should permeate all that you do today and help you through.

Prayer Starter

Lord Jesus, it's a wonderful thing to realize that You are thinking about me all day today. Knowing that I am so important and loved by You, fills my heart with joy and peace. Thank you, Lord. You'll be in my thoughts today as well. AMEN

"Check Up"

1. How have you believed the lie that God is mean and only wants to punish you?

_____

_____

2. In what ways has this view of God caused you to focus on the negative and judgmental?

_____

_____

3. How can changing your view of how God relates to you help you in your life?

_____

_____

4. What observations did you make today while focusing on today's statement: God is thinking good thoughts about me today?

_____

_____

_____

_____

_____

_____

Prayer Starter

Lord, as I look over this day, I can see Your good thoughts toward me. It has strengthened me. It has supported me. I realize I am not alone and that You have a loving plan for my life. Thank You. AMEN

Day Thirty Two

Morning

Positive Statement for the Day:

I Will Roll Back The Stone So God Can Move

John 11:38-44

Then Jesus, the anger again welling up within him, arrived at the tomb. It was a simple cave in the hillside with a slab of stone laid against it. Jesus said, "Remove the stone."
The sister of the dead man, Martha, said, "Master, by this time there's a stench. He's been dead four days!"

Jesus looked her in the eye. "Didn't I tell you that if you believed, you would see the glory of God?"

Then, to the others, "Go ahead, take away the stone."

They removed the stone. Jesus raised his eyes to heaven and prayed, "Father, I'm grateful that you have listened to me. I know you always do listen, but on account of this crowd standing here I've spoken so that they might believe that you sent me."

Then he shouted, "Lazarus, come out!" And he came out, a cadaver, wrapped from head to toe, and with a kerchief over his face.

Jesus told them, "Unwrap him and let him loose."

Wow, what a dramatic story John relays to us. It really shows the heart of the Savior. Jesus wanted to do a huge miracle. His buddy Lazarus had died and Jesus was going to show the power of God over death by raising Lazarus from the grave.

There was only one problem. Jesus asked the people to roll the stone away from the tomb. There were comments like, "He's been dead four days," or "Lord, he stinks by now." Finally they roll it away, reluctantly, and Jesus is able to change the situation.

Do you need a miracle? Is there something in your life that needs to be changed? Is something "dead" or "stinky" in your life that is causing you grief?

Perhaps you need to move a "stone" away from the situation so God can work.

He wants to raise you and this problem up from depths of sorrow into new life. What area of unbelief, sin, or fear is keeping God from moving in your life?

Confess it! Move it out of the way. Get that stone out of here so God can do the miraculous in your life. Don't stay dead, but come alive. You can only be "loosed" when you take away the stone that is keeping the miracle from happening. Don't delay any longer. Let Jesus speak words of life over your situations.

Prayer Starter

God of life, I need Your touch today. I have a real need for a miracle. I have "dead" issues in my life that need Your life-giving touch. So, Father, I confess my lack of faith, my sins, and my fear. I remove those stones so You can show up in resurrection power. AMEN

"Check Up"

1. Look at your life. Where do you need a life changing miracle?

   _____
   _____

2. What "stone" do you need to remove in order for Jesus to speak life into your circumstances?

   _____
   _____

3. What excuses have you been giving that have kept you from removing the stone?

   _____
   _____

4. What observations did you make today while focusing on today's statement: I will roll back the stone so God can move?

   _____
   _____
   _____
   _____
   _____
   _____

Prayer Starter

Thank You, Lord, for showing me how I have been blocking Your miracle power in my life. I realize You want to help me and bring glory to the Father at the same time. Give me strength to move the stone. Help me to keep it moved and not to roll back in place. AMEN

Day Thirty Three

Morning

Positive Statement for the Day:

I Will Recognize GIGO

2 Corinthians 10:3-6

The world is unprincipled. It's dog-eat-dog out there! The world doesn't fight fair. But we don't live or fight our battles that way—never have and never will.
The tools of our trade aren't for marketing or manipulation, but they are for demolishing that entire massively corrupt culture.
We use our powerful God-tools for smashing warped philosophies, tearing down barriers erected against the truth of God, fitting every loose thought and emotion and impulse into the structure of life shaped by Christ.
Our tools are ready at hand for clearing the ground of every obstruction and building lives of obedience into maturity.

GIGO is a computer term that means, "Garbage In, Garbage Out." It communicates that a computer is only as good as the information the operator puts into it. If you enter false data in the computer (even one number wrong) the results of the computation will be off.

For you, GIGO means that you have to guard what you put into your mind and spirit. If you put garbage in, then that's what is going to come out.

Just like a sponge, your spirit will pour out whatever you have put into it. When you squeeze a sponge that has been soaking in water, then water is what will come out. Don't expect soda or milk.

So it is with you. When life squeezes you, what you have soaked in will come out. When the pressures of daily living are upon you, whatever you have allowed to take residence in your mind is what will come to surface.

With that in mind, you must protect yourself.

You have to guard what you watch on TV or on movies, the music you listen to, the books you read, the magazines you look at, the sites you visit on the internet, the people you hang out with, the kind of jokes you listen to, and the type of language you allow to be used in your presence.

Decide today to review the input process of your mind. See what you are allowing to continually build within you. Watch out for the garbage! Take the garbage out, don't let it take residence in you and begin to spoil and stink up your life and attitudes.

Ask the Holy Spirit for help. Whatever garbage you have allowed to pile up in your life, have Him assist you in taking it to the dump. Spiritually renounce those things and replace them with good thoughts and actions.

Prayer Starter
Dear Heavenly Father, help me guard my mind today. I need Your Holy Spirit to be the sentinel of my mind so that I may produce a life that is pleasing to You. AMEN

"Check Up"

1. How can you see that the process of GIGO has worked in your past?

_____

_____

2. What areas of "garbage in" has the Holy Spirit revealed for you to consider?

_____

_____

3. Exactly how will you stop the flow of that garbage into your mind?

_____

_____

4. What observations did you make today while focusing on today's statement: I will recognize GIGO?

_____

_____

_____

_____

_____

Prayer Starter

This is really going to help, Heavenly Father. Thank You for guiding me. I want to keep the flow of garbage from coming into my life. I saw it all around me today. Give me the fortitude to resist the garbage I've become so accustomed to putting into my mind. I know it won't be easy, but with Your help, I can do it. AMEN

Day Thirty Four

Morning

Positive Statement for the Day:

I Will Minimize The Effect Of Negative People On My Life

Romans 16:17
One final word of counsel, friends. Keep a sharp eye out for those who take bits and pieces of the teaching that you learned and then use them to make trouble. Give these people a wide berth.

1 Corinthians 5:9,11
I wrote you in my earlier letter that you shouldn't make yourselves at home among the sexually promiscuous. I didn't mean that you should have nothing at all to do with outsiders of that sort.
But I am saying that you shouldn't act as if everything is just fine when a friend who claims to be a Christian is promiscuous or crooked, is flip with God or rude to friends, gets drunk or becomes greedy and predatory. You can't just go along with this, treating it as acceptable behavior.

Proverbs 20:19
*Gossips can't keep secrets,
so never confide in blabbermouths.*

Negative people suck the life out of you. You know this. You've experienced it in your life. It is not a surprise by any stretch of the imagination. What is a surprise is that, knowing this, we still choose to allow these negative people to make such an impact on our lives.

You can reduce, if not eliminate, some negative people's influence on your life. You can make the choice. You can decide to decrease your exposure to them. You can diminish the affect you allow their negativity to impact you.

That means you have to guard your mind, your eyes, your ears and your spirit. Stop watching so much negative news on the TV. Don't listen to other people's negative comments. Think positively. Think in faith.

Sometimes you have to love negative people from a distance. You still care for them. You still want the best for them. You still love them. You just need to limit their impact on your disposition.

You have to build your own positive reinforcement. You decide who you hang out with, who you listen to, and who has influence on your life.

The power is in your hands to not allow the negative to suck the life out of you. You decide to place your focus on faith, expectation, and the positivity of the Gospel of Jesus Christ.

Prayer Starter
I choose, Father, to minimize and reduce the impact of negative people on my life. I will remain positive and forward looking by Your help and grace. AMEN

"Check Up"

1. What people in your life are a constant negative influence that drags your spirit down?

_____

_____

2. How can you take charge and limit their negative exposure towards you?

_____

_____

3. Loving negative people from a distance isn't easy. How will you accomplish this in your life?

_____

_____

4. What observations did you make today while focusing on today's statement: I will minimize the effect of negative people on my life?

_____

_____

_____

_____

_____

Prayer Starter

Thank You, Lord Jesus, for showing the power that negativity has had in my life. I need Your wisdom as I seek to limit those influences in my life. Help me understand how to love negative people with Your love without subjecting myself to that influence. AMEN

Day Thirty Five

Morning

Positive Statement for the Day:

I Will Surround Myself With Positive People

Hebrews 10:24-25

*Let's see how inventive we can be in encouraging love and
helping out, not avoiding worshiping together as some do but
spurring each other on,
especially as we see the big Day approaching.*

You have a choice. You can decide. It's up to you
who you allow to have an impact on your life. Who you let
speak into your life is totally your decision.

The scales of your attitude will tip one way or the
other, Negative or Positive. Which way they tip depends on
the choices you make in regard to companionship.

The question is will you choose to surround yourself
with negative or positive influences? You get to pick. The
selection is up to you.

Today, make the choice to surround yourself with
positive people. Hang out with others who have an optimistic,
faith filled attitude. Resolve to only focus on permitting
people with an encouraging, affirmative, upbeat view of life to
speak into your life.

Downplay the negative. Don't let depressing, unconstructive people have the power to put you down. Don't let their words determine your attitude.

Make your mind up that only those with a "glass half full" mentality will have the right or opportunity to influence you today. Elect for optimism over pessimism all day today.

When you spend a day like this, it will begin to dramatically change your outlook. You will begin to see the negativity around you. It will make you more creative as you look for the positive people, things, and circumstances.

Being positive in the Christian life is really all about faith. Faith is believing in a positive manner what God and His word say.

This is part of what is meant by, "The just shall live by faith."

That is not just a one-time saving faith. But rather it is a daily, positive, expectation that God will perform His word in your life.

He is in control, and with that promise, you will eventually have a positive outcome.

Prayer Starter

Jesus, bring positive people into my life today. Help me be strong. I don't want to let negative people infect my spirit. I want to be full of faith and possibility. Give me the fortitude I need to guard my spirit from the negative influences of the world and to allow only the good into my heart. AMEN

"Check Up"

1. What unique ways did the Spirit of God show you to minimize the negative and focus on the positive?

_____

_____

2. Who did you have to keep away from today in order to keep positive?

_____

_____

3. How has God shown you the correlation between being positive and living by faith?

_____

_____

4. What observations did you make today while focusing on today's statement: I will surround myself with positive people?

_____

_____

_____

_____

_____

Prayer Starter

Heavenly Father, I know that You want me to be a positive influence on my family, friends and others. I realize now how challenging that can be. Help me, by active faith, live an uplifting life before the world so that they may see the joy You have given me. AMEN

Section 8

MOTIVATED
To Be An Ambassador

.

Day Thirty Six

Morning

Positive Statement for the Day:

I Will Help Someone Else Become Successful

1 Corinthians 12:25-27

The way God designed our bodies is a model for understanding our lives together as a church: every part dependent on every other part, the parts we mention and the parts we don't, the parts we see and the parts we don't.

If one part hurts, every other part is involved in the hurt, and in the healing. If one part flourishes, every other part enters into the exuberance.

You are Christ's body—that's who you are!

\Hebrews 10:24

Let's see how inventive we can be in encouraging love and helping out,

The world in which we live today has been come a "dog-eat-dog" world. Everyone is looking out for number one. Meaning they look out for themselves and put very little thought in how they can help others become successful.

The church, the called out ones of God, should have a different attitude. We are part of the body of Jesus Christ. We are to help one another. When one succeeds, we all succeed.

You can help someone else. You can step out on purpose and do or say something that will help one of your brothers or sisters in the Lord become successful. It only requires that you open your eyes to the opportunities around you.

You can find a way to encourage, lift up, or direct someone in their personal or business life. Perhaps you can help someone make a connection that will help them do well.

Make a conscious effort today to look for those types of opportunities. Give good advice. Create a positive atmosphere that generates faith and hope in someone else's abilities and opportunities.

Your closest Christian friends can be your project. They need assistance in order to achieve or accomplish a goal in their life. You can help. Just look, on purpose, for a way to be a blessing in their life.

Prayer Starter

Open my eyes, Lord. Help me see the ways I can be a blessing to my spiritual family today. Help me look beyond myself and see the needs of others as they struggle to make it. AMEN

"Check Up"

1. Who did you help on the road to success throughout your day today?

   _____

   _____

2. What did you do, specifically, that was positive and faith-building to help them?

   _____

   _____

3. Since you've seen how easy and meaningful this action is, who else can you help succeed?

   _____

   _____

4. What observations did you make today while focusing on today's statement: I will on purpose help someone else become successful?

   _____

   _____

   _____

   _____

   _____

Prayer Starter

Father, I pray for _____, the person I tried to help succeed today. I pray for their continued accomplishment. That the words and actions You guided me to use will build faith in them. May they realize how much You love them and want to bless them. AMEN

Day Thirty Seven

Morning

Positive Statement for the Day:

I Will Find Somebody I Can Be Good To Today

Romans 15:2, 14

Each one of us needs to look after the good of the people around us, asking ourselves, "How can I help?" Personally, I've been completely satisfied with who you are and what you are doing. You seem to me to be well-motivated and well-instructed, quite capable of guiding and advising one another

Galatians 6:6-10

Be very sure now, you who have been trained to a self-sufficient maturity, that you enter into a generous common life with those who have trained you, sharing all the good things that you have and experience. Don't be misled: No one makes a fool of God. What a person plants, he will harvest. The person who plants selfishness, ignoring the needs of others—ignoring God!—harvests a crop of weeds. All he'll have to show for his life is weeds! But the one who plants in response to God, letting God's Spirit do the growth work in him, harvests a crop of real life, eternal life. So let's not allow ourselves to get fatigued doing good. At the right time we will harvest a good crop if we don't give up, or quit. Right now, therefore, every time we get the chance, let us work for the benefit of all, starting with the people closest to us in the community of faith.

Today, you are on a mission. Your mission isn't to just build yourself up or make sure you are number one. Instead you are going to find someone, anyone, that you can reach out to and be good to today.

Everywhere you go today, look for an opportunity to be a "Good Samaritan." Even if it is just a glass of cold water on a hot day, you are going to just be good to people.

Maybe you will open a door for someone carrying a big package, or maybe you'll carry it for them. Perhaps you'll pay for some stranger's meal or coffee.

The possibilities are endless if you are focused on finding them. People need a touch of goodness in their lives. The world needs people who are willing to look beyond their needs and touch someone else, even complete strangers.

Through the power and leading of the Holy Spirit, you can make that difference in your part of the world today.

Prayer Starter
Jesus, develop in me a heart to do good to my fellow man today. Give me opportunities to show the goodness and love of God to others, and the strength to step out and do it. I need the guidance of Your Holy Spirit today. AMEN

"Check Up"

1. What acts of goodness (kindness) are you able to put into your daily routine?

_____

_____

2. How did your random act of goodness today make you feel?

_____

_____

3. How can you expect God to open your eyes to those opportunities more often?

_____

_____

4. What observations did you make today while focusing on today's statement: I will find somebody I can be good to today?

_____

_____

_____

_____

_____

Prayer Starter

I am so grateful, Jesus, that You answered my prayer this morning and opened my eyes to see ways I can be good to others today. I would love to be that type of missionary every day. Will You please implant that type of attitude in my spirit? I feel closer to You and more like You when I do this. Amen

Day Thirty Eight

Morning

Positive Statement for the Day:

I Choose To See The Best In Other People

Acts 4:36

Joseph, called by the apostles "Barnabas" (which means "Son of Comfort"), a Levite born in Cyprus, sold a field that he owned, brought the money, and made an offering of it to the apostles.

Acts 9:26-27

Back in Jerusalem he tried to join the disciples, but they were all afraid of him. They didn't trust him one bit. Then Barnabas took him under his wing. He introduced him to the apostles and stood up for him, told them how Saul had seen and spoken to the Master on the Damascus Road and how in Damascus itself he had laid his life on the line with his bold preaching in Jesus' name.

Acts 15:37-39

Barnabas wanted to take John along, the John nicknamed Mark. But Paul wouldn't have him; he wasn't about to take along a quitter who, as soon as the going got tough, had jumped ship on them in Pamphylia. Tempers flared, and they ended up going their separate ways: Barnabas took Mark and sailed for Cyprus

OK, we've all heard it, but let me ask you again. Do you view the glass as half full or half empty? Do you see the positive around you, or do you focus on the negative? When you see someone, it's only natural that you view them through your own internal senses.

Regretfully, we have been programmed to judge that person without even knowing them or their situation.

Today, you are going to rise above that judgment mentality. You are going to see beyond the externals. You are going to choose to see the best in other people.

Remember, God has saved and changed you. You are not who you used to be because of the grace of God.

Choose to see the possibilities in others. See them as God sees them. He knows their potential. He loves them. He wants them to succeed and become active in His church. He has a desire for them to cast their cares on Him, because He cares for them.

You can change your view of the world, one person at a time.

Prayer Starter

I thank You, Lord, for seeing the best in me, when everyone else around could only see the worst in me. Prompt me through Your Spirit today to choose to only see the best, the positive, and the possibilities in others. AMEN

"Check Up"

1. What stereotypes or judgments has God revealed need to be changed in your life?

_____

_____

2. What positive steps will you take in order for God to help you change?

_____

_____

3. Who do you see differently now that you have focused on the best?

_____

_____

4. What observations did you make today while focusing on today's statement: I choose to see the best in other people?

_____

_____

_____

_____

_____

Prayer Starter

Today was not so easy, Lord. I have realized that I still have stereotypes and judgments that need to be dealt with. I want to see the potential in others. I know I should look beyond appearances and externals. Give me the desire and the power to change. AMEN

Day Thirty Nine

Morning

Positive Statement for the Day:

I Will Give Compliments Freely Today

---

1 Thessalonians 5:11
Build up hope so you'll all be together in this, no one left out, no one left behind. I know you're already doing this; just keep on doing it.

Ephesians 4:28-30

Did you use to make ends meet by stealing?

Well, no more! Get an honest job so that you can help others who can't work.

Watch the way you talk. Let nothing foul or dirty come out of your mouth. Say only what helps, each word a gift.

Don't grieve God. Don't break his heart. His Holy Spirit, moving and breathing in you, is the most intimate part of your life, making you fit for himself. Don't take such a gift for granted.

Let's say you are going on vacation. You search for the best deal and go to the coast and have a wonderful time. The room is clean, the weather is nice, and the service is good. You are rested and refreshed. You have a good time. You may tell someone else about the place where you stayed, but most of us wouldn't just go back online and fill out a positive review of our stay.

But let one person on the staff be rude to us. You let house cleaning forget to put fresh towels in you room, and you wham the review site before you even leave.

We live in a selfish world. Everything is about "me." We want to be recognized. We desire the applause of the crowd. We crave attention. Everyone longs to be complimented.

That being the case, it goes counter-cultural to be giving compliments, especially a lot them; or to be looking for ways to give out praise and accolades.

So for most of us, giving compliments doesn't come easily. Maybe we didn't receive a lot of them ourselves, but they don't just flow off the tongue easily.

Life and death are in the power of the tongue. Too often we fall into the mindset of the world to openly criticize and rarely, if ever, compliment others. Today is compliment day!

Today you are going to look for ANYTHING you can verbally compliment.

Prayer Starter

Father, even when You created everything, You looked and said, "It is good." Give me that attitude today. Show me ways, all day, that I can freely give compliments to other and brighten their day. AMEN

"Check Up"

1. How difficult 'was it to find someone you could offer a compliment to today?

_____

_____

2. How many people were you able to compliment during the course of the day?

_____

_____

3. What was the reaction of those you complimented today?

_____

_____

4. What observations did you make today while focusing on today's statement: I will give compliments freely today?

_____

_____

_____

_____

_____

Prayer Starter

Lord, I never realized how easy it could be to make a difference in someone's day. You used me to lift them up, and as a result I felt invigorated. I'm sure You were pleased as well. Thank You for using me that way. I want to experience that more. Help me see every opportunity to compliment others. AMEN

Day Forty

Morning

Positive Statement for the Day:

Today I Will Make Everyone I Meet Feel Important

Romans 12:9-18

Love from the center of who you are; don't fake it.

Run for dear life from evil; hold on for dear life to good. Be good friends who love deeply; practice playing second fiddle.

Don't burn out; keep yourselves fueled and aflame. Be alert servants of the Master, cheerfully expectant. Don't quit in hard times; pray all the harder. Help needy Christians; be inventive in hospitality.

Bless your enemies; no cursing under your breath. Laugh with your happy friends when they're happy; share tears when they're down. Get along with each other; don't be stuck-up. Make friends with nobodies; don't be the great somebody.

Don't hit back; discover beauty in everyone. If you've got it in you, get along with everybody.

Everyone strives for meaning in their life. They want to know that they are important to someone else. They desire a purpose for their life. As children we always dreamed of being successful and important. We played like we were the star or the hero.

Today, your challenge will be to focus on making everyone you meet feel important, like they really matter. Treat them with respect. Honor them. Hold them in high esteem. Be kind to them.

Everyone is a candidate for your blessing today. The person at the store, work, the fast food place, at the coffee shop, your family and friends; they all deserve to feel important.

You can do this by deferring to them in many ways. Let them go first. Let them decide about lunch. Let them know how much they mean to you and how it would be terrible if they were not around you.

Try their idea today. Let them talk more (and really listen to what they are saying). In short, let the focus be on the positive influence and opportunity for THEM.

Prayer Starter

Lord, I know in my mind that You created man in Your image. I know that everyone has needs, but I usually focus on my own. I'm sorry for being selfish. Help me make everyone I meet today feel important. AMEN

"Check Up"

1. Who did you surprise by making them feel more important?

_____

_____

2. What creative ways did God show you that you could accomplish your task today?

_____

_____

3. Once you made someone feel important, how did they respond to you?

_____

_____

4. What observations did you make today while focusing on today's statement: Today I will make everyone I meet feel important?

_____

_____

_____

_____

_____

Prayer Starter
I know that Your word says that You so loved us that You gave Your one and only Son for us. True love gives and I realize that now. As I gave today by making someone else feel important, I understood a fraction of what You experience each time You accept us as Your children. Thank You for that, Lord Jesus. AMEN

Afterword

Make This One Decision To
Change Your Life And Eternal Destiny

As you have read through this book, you have seen that our focus is based on a relationship with God through His Son, Jesus Christ.

Though I believe there is intrinsic value in the material you studied, the real value is spiritual. In my opinion the first and best decision you can make is to become a follower of Jesus. When you pursue His presence He gives you the strength to make other 1% changes.

The notion of many people today is that they will try and clean up their life before they turn toward God. This is a mistaken concept. You come to Him just as you are and ask for His assistance in changing your life.

If you want to see the truths of this book really come alive in you, make that decision today. Talk to God. Admit that you need His help. Believe that He wants to be a part of your life.

Understand that He loves you so much. He actually sent Jesus to pay the eternal penalty for you so that you can spend eternity with Him. If you are serious about seeking after God, pray this prayer with all sincerity and God will answer and a new life will begin within you.

Dear God. I need your help. I know that You love me and sent Jesus to take my punishment. I am willing to follow You and to make the decision to change with Your help. Thank You, Lord, for hearing my prayer. AMEN.

Make This Powerful Decision

The word of God promises that for those who surrender their lives to Him, He will baptize them in His Holy Spirit and they will receive power.

This promise is not for just anyone, but to those who are His disciples. If you have become a disciple of Jesus and desire to live a holy and powerful life, ask God for this outpouring.

Holiness is a state of being, not adherence to a set of rules. Almighty God desires to do a cleansing work in your spirit. He even says, "Be holy, as I am holy."

Begin this journey by totally surrendering every facet of your life to Him. Don't just share your life with Him, give Him total control.

Daily yield every aspect of your being to His control. Watch as He is faithful to infuse you with great and mighty power. Learn to daily walk in the Spirit and to exercise both the fruit and the gifts of the Spirit. Prayer for Holy Spirit Baptism:

Heavenly Father, You have promised the out-pouring of Your Spirit to me. I run to Jesus, the Author and Finisher of my faith for this experience. I need Your power. I desire Your guidance. I am desperate for a cleansing of my carnal nature and appetites. I trust You, by faith, to fill me with such love and power as to change my nature. I totally and unequivocally surrender both everything I have and also all that I am to You. Thank You, Lord, for hearing my prayer. AMEN

LOOK FOR THESE TITLES BY
DR. LONNIE E. RILEY
COMING SOON.

SCHEDULE

DR. & MRS. RILEY

FOR YOUR EVENTS

Dr. Riley is open for scheduling for the following events:

- ➢ Book Signings

- ➢ Speaking engagements for your group/congregation

- ➢ Concerts

For information on scheduling visit

www.fmintl.org

ABOUT THE AUTHOR

Lonnie E. Riley, B.A., M.A., D.Min., is the Executive Director of Freedom Ministries International. He is a prolific author, song writer and teacher

The scope of his ministry includes church planting (5 congregations), Senior and Associate pastorates, evangelist, author, and teacher.

His family consists of his wife, Kimberly and 3 grown sons; Jason (wife Kymberly), Joshua and Randall.

Dr. and Mrs. Riley presently make their home in Myrtle Beach, SC.